WEIRD WALK

WANDERINGS AND WONDERINGS THROUGH THE BRITISH RITUAL YEAR

Weird Walk
First published in the UK and USA in 2023 by
Watkins, an imprint of Watkins Media Limited
Unit 11, Shepperton House, 83–93 Shepperton Road
London N1 3DF

Conceived, researched, written and designed by Weird Walk: Alex Hornsby, James Nicholls and Owen Tromans
Publisher: Fiona Robertson
Copyeditor: Sue Lascelles
Proofreading and index: Jo Penning
Illustrator: Mr Gordo
Production: Uzma Taj

A CIP record for this book is available from the British Library

ISBN: 978-1-78678-682-1 (Hardback)
ISBN: 978-1-78678-731-6 (eBook)

10 9 8 7 6 5 4 3 2 1

Printed in China

www.weirdwalk.co.uk

www.watkinspublishing.com

CONTENTS

AUTUMN

WINTER

FOREWORD

Two books bestrode my childhood, and made me the man I am:
The Magic Bridle, a collection of British and Irish myths retold by the
folklorist Forbes Stuart, which ignited my six-year-old imagination in
1974, and *Mysterious Britain* by Janet and Colin Bord, published two
years earlier, and part of a then burgeoning bookseller phenomenon of
often unreliable earth mysteries compendiums. Nonetheless, they set
this particular boy off, seeking out ancient sites whenever possible. Now
everything has wilted but I still have calves of iron, and I can identify
the outline of a hilltop earthwork from a moving car on a motorway as
surely as a falcon seeing a field mouse five hundred feet below. One day
someone will appreciate me.

Through childhood and adolescence I worked towards my
mysterious targets, assembling my own apostolic archive of similar but
unrelated seventies texts, light on detail and heavy on conjecture. Where
were these places of power? I would see them! "You and your old ruins!"
my gran would cluck dismissively, as I politely requested we broke our
Morris Marina journey southwest to the caravan site, at Stanton Drew
or Glastonbury. And when I stumbled in my cub-scout shorts to find
the Longstone Barrow, which I had only seen in a blurred pamphlet
picture, my divorcee dad waited patiently in a car at the bottom of
Challacombe Common, counting down the functional alcoholic hours
to opening time. God bless him! Today I feel his pain. But we were all
weird walking blind back then, columns of confused men with their
hands on the shoulders of the equally confused man in front, seeking
silhouettes of standing stones in the mists of imaginary moors.

And then, in the closing hours of the twentieth century, came Julian
Cope's *The Modern Antiquarian*, a landmark practical tome for the
would-be site-seeker, served up in its own mud-proof slipcase, synthesising
archaeology, folklore, grid references, helpful full-colour maps, parking
advice and a small smidgeon of Cope's own eccentric interpretations,
often later validated by reluctantly admiring academics. The stones were
stages! Rock and roll! It was a game-changer, and Cope opened up the
crack in the Devil's Grave of our folkloric landscape to all, like the wizard

7

of Alderley Edge. "Hello, Julian!" said some graffiti, knife-clawed in 1999 into the information sign at Belas Knap Long Barrow; and I hoped such sites were not about to become a victim of their own popularity. In the end, it was climate change and the unfreezing of the peat that caused the Ring of Brodgar to rock, not the writings of a rock star.

But Weird Walk is not *The Modern Antiquarian*. If anything, the three Weird Walkers, whoever they may be, have returned the love of folk tales, ancient sites and the pleasurable perambulations that lead one to their locations even more defiantly to the realm of the gentleman and gentlewoman amateurs who first documented them. The sensibly shod seventeenth-century parson, mapping the megaliths between

funerals and marriages, and the aristocratic antiquary, pleading with some Cornish farmer to spare the collapsed burial chamber whose capstone he had earmarked for a pigsty wall, would recognise the Weird Walkers as kindred spirits. No one knows who they are, or what they are doing. But their legacy remains. Are they bound together in blood by the call of the Way of the Weird Walk? Or are they just trying to escape mundane reality by adding an air of significance to what may essentially be extended rural pub crawls with ideas above their station? Just as we may never really know who were the architects of Stonehenge, so the real Weird Walkers remain as opaque as the wizard sages, leaving behind their footprints in Whitman's sands of time.

What we do know is that the three Weird Walkers followed their noses, and were already walking weirdly before it ever occurred to them that their weekend wanderings could become a fanzine, a website and, finally, this book. And yet, in their costly boots and cagoules, they seem to have stumbled into something. It's Halloween 2022 as I write this. I cannot move a sparrow nest in my chimney because the frighteningly warm weather has extended the breeding season apocalyptically; there will be no cold-breath clouds when the children dress as dark spirits and go door to door this night; and four days ago, Thérèse Coffey, this month's Tory Environment Secretary, countered the UN's claims that nothing short of an entire global restructuring of the way we live can save the planet, with a pitiful call to continue to avoid disposable cups. Without understanding we are doomed. But the Weird Walkers walk the landscape in the shadows of the seasons as we used to experience them before they blurred, reminding us of how we once measured out the increments of our humanity, and etched it into rock and earth, in the annual cycles of rotting and rebirth. When we lose this knowledge, we are lost. We're probably lost anyway to be honest, but fuck it, let's go down drunk and walking weird.

Like those earlier antiquarians, the Weird Walkers are not professionals. They do not curate or catalogue. They will not be found in the museum office or the heritage centre hub. Instead, they offer, almost idly, thoughts and impressions on the sites they visit, shot through with references to the popular culture of their own times, and fall short of some great scientific revelatory overview; for that is not their ultimate goal, even though it may be their unintended consequence. Instead, they inspire you, the reader, to turn off your television set and go and do some weird walking instead. They have re-enchanted themselves. Can you be re-enchanted too?

The idea that the game of golf is "a good walk ruined" is popularly, but probably wrongly, attributed to Mark Twain. Well, try this on for size, aphorism accumulators of the future: Weird Walk – it's a good walk weird.

— Stewart Lee, writer/clown,
Stoke Newington, October 2022

PREAMBLE

"It was seen that the seasons were annual, that they went round in a ring; and because that annual ring was long in revolving, great was man's hope and fear in the winter, great his relief and joy in the spring."
—Jane Ellen Harrison, *Ancient Art and Ritual*

At the close of the last ice age, over 12,000 years ago, people walked to a place that would one day become known as Great Britain. This place, part of a North Atlantic archipelago of more than 6,000 islands, is, in one sense, the subject of this book. Its compact geography is frequently one of intense beauty; and from Hampshire's gentle, sun-dappled valleys to the thunderous roar of Sutherland's waters, its radical diversity is capable of springing wondrous surprises.

But within this landscape there are ghosts. Those early ramblers who ended our islands' millennia of abandonment to the frigid elements would have brought beliefs and stories with them. Perhaps they explained in mythological terms the changes wrought by an erratically warming climate; perhaps they even knew that other humans had lived here long ago, before the ice. Later, their descendants and those migrants who followed in their footsteps would add their own tales. This is the land of Cheddar Man and the Beaker people, of Celts, Romans, Saxons, Vikings, Normans, Scots, Irish, English, Welsh and today a blend of myriad nationalities and ethnicities. Stories seep into the landscape, altering how it is perceived and haunting successive generations in different, unpredictable ways. Britain has, as folklorist Tina Paphitis shows us, accreted many ghosts; and these histories and mysteries – these revenants that haunt and fascinate us – can still be accessed in our environment, visible in the landscape and present in the folklore, outside of museum walls.[1]

Over thousands of years, prehistoric people imposed their will upon nature – creating moorland, clearing boulders and raising stunning megaliths. They transformed their environment, yet also venerated it. Through offerings in sacred waters and in the depths of flint mines, gifts were given in return for nature's abundance. Day followed night and spring followed winter. Life rose from the soil. Whatever our best guesses about pagan British spirituality, we can be confident that the land played a key role. The ground below was as important as any gods in the sky above. The connection to nature was assured, immovable and, over time, came to be marked and honoured in a seasonal pattern of rituals and festivals, some following the movement of the moon and sun through the sky, others synchronised with the agricultural cycle.

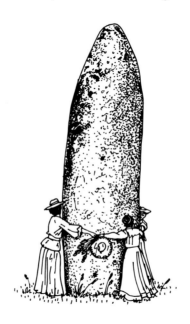

From the Mesolithic hunter-gatherer to the medieval ploughboy, pre-industrial people were connected to the changing seasons in a way few of us are today. In cities, with their air conditioning and constant light, we can sometimes feel suspended in a continual non-season, a metamodern limbo of everything-all-the-time, where seasonal change is only evidenced by the availability of different novelty coffee drinks. The old markers of time still exist, however. Britain's revenant spirit can be found, often off the beaten track, down country lanes and in the fields and woodlands. Just like our stone circles and hill figures, which serve to remind us of earlier times, we are haunted by the customs and rituals of our ancestors – the May pageants, the wassails, the 'Obby 'Osses and morris dances; these all form part of the deep resource of folklore and enchantment available to us all. The old ways have not entirely disappeared. Perhaps it is within these strange echoes of the ritual year, within the landscape and the lore, that we can find reconnection, a healthy dose of natural magic as a corrective to relentless capitalist realism.

How then to access this alternate world, this echo of Albion? We would suggest that it is best done by walking. To truly experience the histories and mysteries embedded within our landscape, getting out and about for a wander is hard to beat. It is how weird walking was born, after all.

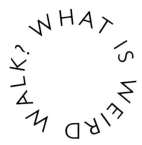

WHAT IS WEIRD WALK?

Formed in the hinterland between the bucolic and the eerie, Weird Walk began as three friends walking an ancient trackway across southern England while wearing incorrect footwear. Being out in the countryside for extended periods, away from screens and distractions, not only refreshed our brains but sparked a creative enthusiasm for the countless stories in the landscape that we yomped across. Without a clear plan, we spent three transformative days and nights on the Ridgeway trail, stopping off at Neolithic burial chambers, sacred hills and Iron Age earthworks. We misread maps, slept in haunted pubs, drank local ale and drank in local lore, all the while becoming aware that the further from the towns and cities we walked, the wider the temporal boundaries grew. Here was the land of Silbury Hill and Avebury stone circle, of Wayland the Smith and the great Uffington White Horse, whose annual scouring is a true pagan survival; here also was the land of the Druids, the first farming communities, the last Saxon kings and countless age-old folk tales. It was a potent path indeed, and the trip soon led to others.

Within these pages we present our findings in the form of a folkloric rambling guide; a gazetteer of the physical, historical and magical landscapes of these isles, and the customs and traditions that rose around them. It is our hope that by pursuing an active engagement with the landscape, by walking within this strange place we call home, more folks will feel what we felt: a returning balance, a sense of renewed optimism for the future informed by a mythic re-enchantment – a pagan power-up, perhaps? This is not a comprehensive survey of the ancient sites of Britain, nor is it an exhaustive field guide to traditional festivals and calendar customs. Rather, it serves as a way in, a conduit, for the curious wanderer with the instinctive understanding that a journey backwards through time is best taken on foot.

RE-ENCHANTMENT
AND THE
RITUAL YEAR

In Britain today we live in thrall to timetables and technology, our lives increasingly scheduled and surveilled. Much of the population live in towns and cities (83 per cent as of 2019),[2] disconnected from the rural lives of our ancestors. The contrast between our urban, rational and highly networked lives and the lives of people just fifty years ago, is remarkable. Cast the timeline back further and it becomes increasingly difficult to process. In the centuries that have passed since the Christianisation of the heathen hordes, we have almost entirely traded magic for science. Nature and goddess worship are, at best, treated as New Age or "alternative"; certainly not to be taken seriously, but filed away with healing crystals and charmed amulets. The discussion of ley lines and earth mysteries typically provokes derision or ridicule. The accepted notion in our modern present is that any kind of magical thinking, or in other words enchantment, belongs to an older age, to a time of superstition. We are conditioned to push back against any sense of innocent bewilderment with nature and its mysteries; we are taught to accept enchantment as naïve.

If urban and suburban surroundings reinforce this desacralised thinking, it follows that a shift to more pastoral realms might be a first step towards opening the door to re-enchantment. The truly ancient sacred sites are huge repositories of myth and memory, their design and placement in the land deliberately calculated to inspire awe. These semiconductors of enchantment are typically found in more remote parts of the landscape, on rugged moors or windswept hillsides, and are generally best accessed on foot. If cities have their psychogeographers and the edgelands their deep topographers, then the countryside has its weird walkers. The sense of connection to something timeless and quietly powerful felt when hiking out to a stone circle or a dolmen is compelling. As writer John Higgs observed, "In modern business districts, such as Canary Wharf or central Milton Keynes, the present is all that matters, and the near future is all that is thought about. If we go to a place that is thousands of years old, such as the Giza pyramids or Stonehenge, the shift in our sense of ourselves is pronounced. As individuals we become insignificant, but at the same time the story we are part of becomes much greater."[3] For us, the pathway to a more optimistic future must include re-enchantment. And the most efficient route there starts by establishing a meaningful connection to the land, to nature and, most importantly, the seasons.

The ritual year is often conceptualised as a wheel, its cyclical nature capturing perfectly the birth, death and renewal that can be inferred from the seasons. This sacred ring has its roots in a range of ancient observances practised in pre-Christian Europe. As far back as the Bronze Age, the remarkable Nebra sky disc depicted the movements of heavenly bodies on a literal circular artefact. Following the early work of Jacob Grimm, neopagans developed the wheel of the year as we now know it in the twentieth century, drawing on Gaelic rites (the fire festivals of Samhain, Imbolc, Beltane and Lughnasadh), and including four further festivals in the form of the solstices and equinoxes. Mythology was important here – when the Wiccan Aidan Kelly coined the term "Mabon" in 1970 for the ancient practice of observing the autumn equinox, he was referencing Mabon ap Modron, an important figure in Welsh legend. The wheel is a powerful means by which to frame many other seasonal customs that take place in Britain, creating a rich tapestry of interconnected rituals and stories.

Although the wheel of the year itself is a relatively modern construct, these markers in time, and the impulses that underlie them, are undeniably ancient. Indeed, many pagan festivals remain embedded within notable days of the Christian calendar, like standing stones embedded in the crypt of a parish church. As Europe was Christianised, the pagans' high days and holy days were adapted. Imbolc, for example, became St Brigid's Day, and Yule, of course, is now associated with Christmas. Celebrations continued in a different form. (A selection of observances is listed at the start of each season in this book to give a sense of the rich variety enacted across Britain.)

Pre-industrial people throughout history would recognise the concept of time as a cycle, and they would witness this cycle profoundly, indeed spiritually, in the seasonal change all around them. If we are to combat the climate change that is disrupting our seasons, perhaps we must also heed the call to embrace viscerally the natural world and its rhythms. Even if only for the moments spent hiking out to a long barrow or ancient oak, such reconnection can raise our awareness of humanity's inextricable link to nature. The added benefits of a good ramble to mental and physical health are obvious, but, for us, it is the elements of myth and magic that provide the necessary enhancements to our trips, taking things further, into another realm.

THE CONSOLATION
OF HAUNTOLOGY

In the same way that magical thinking has been marginalised in our society, the general forward progress of culture itself has diminished dramatically in recent years. In the post-postmodern Britain of the twenty-first century, we find ourselves living in a time where we have difficulty expressing a clear sense of a lived present. Even in the late 1980s, the political scientist Francis Fukuyama could assert that we were reaching the end of history.[4]

Fukuyama was discussing the victory of liberal democracy and capitalism in the last century's battle for global dominance of competing political ideologies, but bound up in that was his chillingly accurate prediction that "in the post-historical period there will be neither art nor philosophy, just the perpetual caretaking of the museum of human history. I can feel in myself, and see in others around me, a powerful nostalgia for the time when history existed."[5] This became manifest in the retro recycling of culture throughout the 1990s. Writing in 2011, music critic Simon Reynolds took it a step further, observing that the 2000s were "about every other previous decade happening again all at once: a simultaneity of pop time that abolishes history while nibbling away at the present's own sense of itself as an era with a distinct identity and feel".[6]

Influential writer and philosopher Mark Fisher doubled down, asserting that the primary characteristic of twenty-first-century culture is simply twentieth-century culture accessed via faster distribution systems and viewed on higher definition screens. The slow cancellation of the future, as Fisher terms it, was upon us.[7] Ubiquitous anachronism in high-resolution colour with no bandwidth restrictions sounds great on paper, but if the future has been cancelled and the present lacks meaning, maybe now more than ever we should be looking towards the past for clues from the ancients that hint at ways we can return to radical thinking, visions of utopia and a synchronicity with nature.

The standing stones of the Neolithic exert a strong gravitational pull on us. Their atemporality, the sense that they are outside of time, coupled with the impenetrable purpose of their existence, casts a subtle but powerful spell. In the work of Jacques Derrida – the French philosopher who first coined the term "hauntology" – the persistence in the cultural psyche of past events is characterised as an uncanny disruption. Memories of the past and unfulfilled ideologies recurring in the present are troubling spectres, a disturbance to the current timeline and, therefore, a challenge to the future. For us, this lack of temporal cohesion is what draws us in; we welcome the disjunctures in time as a form of enchantment and a means to connect to a deeper sense of place.

Just like those inscrutable old stones, standing buried and unburied simultaneously, folk customs and rituals represent too the spectre of our pagan past. Annual events such as the Abbots Bromley Horn Dance in Staffordshire or the Marshfield Mummers' Play in Gloucestershire exist out of time: incongruous relics of the past repeating themselves in the present. These rites of uncertain provenance practised by our ancestors for hundreds, some say thousands, of years persist in small pockets throughout the land. As charming and quaint as maypoles and corn dollies might seem on the surface, below the Merrie England façade it is possible to perceive something wilder, more primal. The seasonal rituals functioned to propitiate the spirit of the season, to give thanks and make humble offerings in the hope of continued abundance. As *Wicker Man* director Robin Hardy described it, "A world where if you do nice things for the gods, they will do nice things for you."[8] The enduring existence of the calendar customs, and indeed the invention of new ones, clearly speaks to the ongoing desire to anchor oneself to a more earthbound spirituality, to retain a sense – even if only performatively – of a symbiotic, give-and-take relationship with nature, and to honour a tradition, even when the origins of that tradition are obscure or lost altogether.

The term hauntology conjures a nebulous collection of meanings, but the question we ask (and seek to explore within these pages) is what it means to deploy a hauntological perspective as a way of actively engaging with the British landscape. Can we, in a sense, loop back to radical times or moments in history where a more utopian, enchanted future might have been conceivable? In connecting with the folk memories still present in the landscape, can we visualise a more desirable future? Can that which exists no longer influence what is not yet?

However, looking backwards cannot simply be a nostalgic reframing of the past. In fact, it is necessary to acknowledge that the agrarian way of life of our ancestors would have been extremely hard, especially when compared to our lives today. It is easy to re-imagine pre-modern, rural lives in overly sentimental terms, as an arcadian time before the Industrial Revolution and the "dark satanic mills". The truth is life was often exceedingly harsh – toiling in the fields in savage British weather, scratching out subsistence, raising animals to sell and to slaughter, fending off disease. It was a visceral confrontation with nature on a daily basis. Even more reason, then, to acknowledge and celebrate the natural cycle of life. The festivals and customs not only marked the time in the calendar when certain annual milestones were reached, they had a remarkable value as a means of reinforcing the bonds of the community, and no doubt served an invaluable function as an emotional release. A community that wassails together, stays together.

The journeys presented here represent our exploration of this hauntological quest. By walking the ancient pathways, visiting the sacred sites, and immersing ourselves in the folklore and customs of these isles, we hope to fan the faint embers of magic that still smoulder in the grate and conjure that elusive temporal trackway of history and mystery, a route that bypasses nostalgia and leads us back towards optimism and re-enchantment.

HOW TO USE THE WALKING NOTES IN THIS BOOK

Each location in this book is accompanied by walking notes. The notes include nearby sites, local knowledge relevant to the weird walker, and possible rambling routes. We recommend using the Ordnance Survey app (OS Maps Premium) to map your own walks inspired by these notes. The grid references given in the text will work with the OS app or paper maps. The number of the relevant OS paper map is also given.

DISCLAIMER

We have visited all of the sites in this book and have endeavoured to make our notes as accurate as possible. Rambling should be an enjoyable experience but, as with all activities in the outdoors, there is a degree of risk. We accept no responsibility for any loss or damage to personal property, personal accident, injury or public liability when visiting the sites or routes outlined in this book. We cannot be held responsible for inaccuracies resulting from changes in the landscape, or to routes, over time.

SAFETY

Always plan your visits, checking access and rights of way. Seek permission before visiting sites on private land. In our experience, it pays to check the weather and plan ahead with clothing, bottles of water and snacks. A paper map and compass are always useful in case your phone dies. Where sites are more remote, walking with a pal is sensible. Take care when a route involves road walking, and wear reflective clothing. Whenever walking on the coast, be sure to check the tides. Some sites are located in mountainous terrain, so be aware of steep drops and other hazards. Not all sites or routes will be suitable for children and/or dogs.

SPRING

Everything begins in spring, and every spring everything begins again. Although often an unpredictable opening, when sunshine can sit alongside squall, spring always shows us its direction of travel — towards warmth and light.

We see this at Pentre Ifan, one of our favourite venues to witness the spring equinox, that crucial tipping point of the year. And if the equinox has been welcomed by humans from time immemorial, this feeling of celebration only grows as spring nudges into summer, a transition that birthed the grand festivities of Beltane and May Day. In Padstow, a tradition of rare intensity unites a whole town at this time to joyfully usher in the summer months. Scotland's Glen Lyon hosts a lesser-known rite of spring, practised in a wild and lonely landscape, while visitors to Bix Bottom in Oxfordshire can consider how May Day revels have been demonically inverted on the big screen, rural idyll subverted to reveal a darker, more eldritch countryside.

25

Spring is, of course, a time of wondrous fertility, when nature begins to unfurl. It is now that choruses of skylarks, song thrushes and blackbirds enthusiastically court their mates, and celandine flowers scatter the hedgerows with yellow. The personification of this abundance is the Green Man, who we find hidden in the woods above Wootton Rivers in Wiltshire. Such fertility is also present in the marvellous figure of the Cerne Abbas Giant, looking out, proud as punch, across a landscape rich in meaning and memory.

For pre-industrial people, the springtime changes created a powerful sense of positivity and hope. Perhaps it emboldened folk to participate in such mad capers as the Cooper's Hill Cheese Roll, an exuberant Gloucestershire custom that has retained its lawless edge. More than anything, to walk among the old places in spring is to connect directly with a feeling of optimism. One that can only exist at the beginning of another miraculous cycle.

SELECTED SPRING OBSERVANCES:
· Pace Egg plays in northern England – throughout Easter
· Greenwich Easter Monday Lifting – Easter Monday
· Edinburgh Beltane Fire Festival – 30 April
· Minehead Hobby Horse – main event on 1 May
  (unless 1st is a Sunday)
· Hastings Jack in the Green – May Day bank holiday weekend
· Helston Flora Day – 8 May (unless 8th is a Sunday or Monday)
· Castleton Garland Day – 29 May (unless 29th is a Sunday)
· Great Wishford Grovely Ceremony – 29 May

CERNE ABBAS

A fertility symbol of gigantic proportions watches over a Dorset village

DORSET, ENGLAND (ST 66647 01676)
OS EXPLORER 117

The very presence of the Cerne Abbas Giant is an uncanny disruption of modernity – a conduit to an earlier, weirder time chalked out on Trendle Hill. These priapic proportions have towered over the Dorset countryside for centuries, and although the Giant's precise origins are lost in the mists of time, he is this place's *genius loci*, large and in charge, rooted in the locals' minds and their lore.

Viewing the Giant on a bright spring day, and from the optimum vantage point of a car park off the A352, his powerful presence is enhanced by the sunshine, lending a shimmering quality to his chalky outline. There is something brilliantly punk about him: he lacks the swift, impressionistic lines of the Uffington White Horse or the enigmatic, mystical quality of the Long Man of Wilmington, but his appeal is immediate. His feet twist to the left in the manner of Egyptian figures, while his enormous manhood is flanked by stark ribs, and topped with slightly wonky nipples. An elongated arm runs to the right while the other bears a formidable 37m (121ft) club. The face is curiously framed, with eyebrows and mouth producing a slightly startled expression, as though you have interrupted the colossal geoglyph in a particularly arousing, yet private, cudgel-wielding session.

For many, the Giant is clearly a symbol of fertility and tales have long encouraged hopeful couples to get busy among the chalk. Indeed, on

29

a recent fact-finding visit, two possible adherents of this generative folklore were observed, from a respectable distance, sitting in quiet contemplation within the business end of the naked giant. A living tradition continues on Trendle Hill. Such pagan intentions are backed by the Giant's recently confirmed early medieval date, with a suggestion that he is a representation of the Saxon god Helith.[1] Cerne Abbey once stood close to the figure, and was said to have been built to dissuade locals from worshipping this old god. Moreover, the antiquarian William Stukeley, when writing about the Giant in 1764, noted that he was still referred to as "Helis". Long memories in these parts.

If the Giant himself has become associated with fertility rites, so too has the tranquil Silver Well that springs from the ground a short walk from the figure, down in the village of Cerne Abbas itself. Deep in the burial grounds of what was once Cerne Abbey, this is a place of remarkable stillness – a sacred atmosphere surrounds the well, from which a stream flows strongly in springtime. The ancient stone-

"The face is curiously framed, with eyebrows and mouth producing a slightly startled expression, as though you have interrupted the colossal geoglyph in a particularly arousing, yet private, cudgel-wielding session"

flanked source has attracted much lore over the years; it is said that the iron-rich water aids conception, while girls who pray to St Catherine as they turn around three times will soon find a husband. At the foot of one of the spring's upright stones, an engraved Catherine wheel can be found, and in times long gone a chapel dedicated to the saint stood on the hill above the holy well.

Walking back through the village to the Giant, you'll pass the Giant Inn, one of as many as seventeen pubs that could be found in Cerne in the eighteenth century, when the area was a major brewing centre. Now, three pubs remain, with the Giant Inn being notable for its fine ales and to our knowledge the only pub sign in Britain to feature an erect phallus.

Like the village, the Giant has certainly undergone changes in his long history. Archaeology indicates he may once have been clothed, perhaps had a cloak over his arm and may even have carried a grisly human head in his left hand. His famous member was mysteriously extended to its current impressive size in a 1908 recut of the chalk, which removed his navel in the process. However, this shifting of physique and garb cannot obscure one of the most fascinating aspects of the chap on the hill: his connection to the grand tradition of British giants.

Giants loom large in British lore, their presence in these islands explaining the creation of unusual landscape features and ancient structures, from Wade's Causeway to Fingal's Cave. These giants are often lumbering, irritable and rash, the structures they have left us a result of some petty grudge or fit of temper. The story of the formation of Shropshire's mysterious Wrekin hill between Telford and Shrewsbury, for example, features a particularly testy big lad, with the striking name of Gwendol Wrekin ap Shenkin ap Mynyddmawr. Gwendol had taken umbrage against the inhabitants of the distinctly inoffensive Shrewsbury for reasons known only to giantkind, and had decided to dam the River Severn in order to drown the lot of them. Luckily the giant met a wily cobbler while carrying the massive clod of earth intended to wipe out his Salopian foes, and it was he who persuaded Gwendol the

town was too far away to be worth it. Opening his pack, the cobbler moaned that Shrewsbury was so distant he had worn out an entire pack of footwear on his journey. Suitably dissuaded, Gwendol huffed homewards, but not before he dropped the earth he was carrying, forming the Wrekin in the process.

While often characterised as stupid and vengeful creatures such as Gwendol, some British giants held a more noble pedigree. They are present in many of our islands' founding myths, and are even involved in a tale that explains the name "Albion" itself. Geoffrey of Monmouth's *History of the Kings of Britain* records the tale of thirty Syrian princesses who attempt to murder their unworthy, domineering husbands and, by way of punishment, are put to sea in a rudderless ship. When the sisters reach the shores of a verdant, but seemingly empty, island, they name it Albion in honour of the eldest, Albina. The princesses soon adapt to the simple life, foraging for fruit and trapping animals. But they are not alone in Albion – a race of demons also populates the island, and it is with these creatures that the girls couple, their enormous children becoming the giants of British myth. Years later, when the goddess Diana sends Brutus, the legendary Trojan founder of Britain, on his quest for Albion, she is clear that this is a land "by giants once possess'd; now few remain".[2]

Giants may fill the early pages of British legend, but only the Long Man and the Cerne Abbas Giant still stand on our hillsides. Other massive human hill figures could once be found in Oxford, Cambridge and Portsmouth, but all have long since disappeared. As Diana knew so long ago, the giant is a dying breed, and this only makes old Helith of Trendle Hill, in all his high and fertile strangeness, even more precious and worthy of a visit.

WALKING NOTES

You can park at the Giant's View car park and use this as a base to explore the area. From here you can take a walk straight up to the Giant, or head into the village. The Silver Well can be found at ST 66644 01343, near the remains of Cerne Abbey. The surviving abbey porch and guesthouse are tucked away in an impressive back garden and it's well worth popping a coin in the honesty box for a

visit. From the abbey you can head out on a longer walk to Giant's Hill and its wonderful fringe of woodland. We made this a circular wander by bridging across a field at ST 67263 02521. Slightly further out lies the long-distance Wessex Ridgeway path, which runs right across rural Dorset.

As we note above, there are a few choices for refreshment in Cerne Abbas, but we'd definitely recommend a trip to the Cerne Abbas Brewery. Located on a farm a short drive from the village, the brewery, complete with Giant logo, has restarted the grand brewing tradition in the area.

PENTRE IFAN

A magnificent stone portal in the shadow of the Preseli Hills

PEMBROKESHIRE, WALES (SN 09939 37020)
OS EXPLORER OL35

T he spring equinox marks the turning of the year towards warmth, fertility and life. It's a glorious, celebratory time, and the mighty portal dolmen of Pentre Ifan provides the perfect venue to witness an auspicious equinox sunrise. As the sun illuminates the underside of the dolmen's colossal Millennium Falcon of a capstone, the grey megaliths glow a vibrant orange and you sense a circuit complete. The stones themselves seem to conduct the energy of spring. Soon, light plays across the whole structure, and your attention is drawn to the incredible grace and artistry of this monument: three supporting uprights hold all sixteen tonnes of the capstone in place through the most minimal contact, giving the astonishing impression of levitation. Pentre Ifan is the ultimate expression of the idea of dolmens as "stones that float to the sky".[1] To our eyes this is an extraordinary megalithic sculpture, a feat of design and execution overshadowing any of the twentieth century's celebrated modernist greats. Imagine, then, the intense effect of this Neolithic architectural flex in prehistory, when the built environment was comparatively sparse. Potent stuff indeed.

Dolmens were, for many years, thought to have been covered by a mound and used primarily as burial sites, like other monuments of the early Neolithic such as chambered tombs. Increasingly, scholars have questioned this assumption, pointing to the paucity of excavated human remains and the enormous size of dolmen capstones. As archaeologist Vicki Cummings points out, "Why bother lifting and using a stone that weighed 100 tonnes if it was just going to be covered up? These were monuments that were meant to be seen."[2] Pentre Ifan, positioned as it is with dramatic views up to the Preseli Hills and over the Nevern valley, was surely one of these statement pieces.

If Pentre Ifan was an uncovered dolmen, it may have a real connection to the emergence of spring, especially when we consider its position. Rising above the monument is the magnificent sacred mountain of Carningli, the rock of the angels. The contours of the peak have the effect of a shifting Magic Eye image – one minute they betray a bold moai-like face staring at the sky, and in a blink they transform into a reclining female form. This is the goddess of the mountain that many local people speak of, and the effect of this mind-bending pareidolia cannot have been lost upon the ancients who built Pentre Ifan. Some have suggested that the capstone itself was chosen to represent the mountain.[3] Looking over the mammoth megalith's dips and curves, and then back to Carningli, it's a theory that makes a lot of sense: the mountain is part of the monument. Of course, the idea of a goddess in the landscape reverberates strongly with a seasonal change towards light and growth. For early farmers, the coming spring would be a crucial time and, perhaps, the dolmen provided a gathering place to usher in this planting season.

When it comes to farming, a particular brand of self-sufficiency has always run deep in the Preseli Hills. People have tended livestock and grown crops here for thousands of years, and even after the Second World War many traditional hill-farming methods were still in use. It was this sense of arcadian refuge from modernity that appealed to John Seymour, the environmentalist and author of *The Fat of the Land*, a record of his adventures in self-sufficiency and a deeply influential 1960s tome. *The Fat of the Land* focused on the Seymour family's rural life in Suffolk, but in 1964 they came to live on a farm they had purchased below Carningli. John Seymour loved the magical and often harsh landscape of Pembrokeshire, and he kept up a steady stream of eco-

Self-sufficiency pioneer, John Seymour

conscious self-sufficiency publishing that culminated in the wildly successful *Complete Book of Self-Sufficiency* in 1976. With the movement now noted enough to have its own hit sitcom parody in the form of *The Good Life*, it was the off-grid manual the mainstream could get behind.

Partly inspired by John Seymour's embrace of the Preselis as an agrarian idyll, scores of hippies made their way to Pembrokeshire from the late 1960s onwards. Although conditions were often far from utopian for the newcomers, the area became one of the hotspots of countercultural ruralism. The Incredible String Band and their retinue would even temporarily relocate here in 1968. Rob Young summarises the

psychedelic folk group at this point as "a troupe of wise jesters, whose insights and wit were as preposterous or as revelatory as you wished to make them".[4] They were soon immersed in the mysterious nature of their surroundings and were inevitably drawn to Pentre Ifan, which would feature in their deeply odd film *Be Glad for the Song Has No Ending*. Although starting life as a standard documentary with live performances, the film came to incorporate a kind of mystical pantomime, *The Pirate and the Crystal Ball*, in its second half. This simultaneously daft and mesmerising piece of homebrew cinema was filmed over the course of one hectic Pembrokeshire weekend. In the film, Pentre Ifan hosts a strange ritual performed by the guardians of the crystal ball, "the three fates", and the charismatic dolmen is, of course, the perfect backdrop for this hazy fable.

The longhaired influx to west Wales would continue in the seventies, long after the Incredible String Band had relocated north to their Glen Row HQ in the Scottish Borders. A free festival, Meigan Fayre, was even staged in the Preselis for three years between 1973 and 1975. The poster for the 1975 event asked for volunteers to help bring in the harvest as payment for the use of the farmer's land. But not all of the newcomers would stay on in their Shangri-La to bring in the wheat. The writer Richard King, whose excellent *The Lark Ascending* traces the links between the Seymours and countercultural Preseli, notes that the second-hand shops of Pembrokeshire became rich pickings for acid folk vinyl as the hippies eventually drifted away, many leaving their record collections behind with the self-sufficiency dream.[5]

Communities do still exist in these hills that share John Seymour's anti-consumerist ideals and continue to channel the spirit of those who came to the Preselis in his wake. This place certainly still feels like one where a magical connection to the land is possible. Where wonderful things can grow in difficult earth. Standing at Pentre Ifan on the spring equinox, when winter is truly banished by the rising of the sun, this connection

"This place certainly still feels like one where a magical connection to the land is possible. Where wonderful things can grow in difficult earth"

is amplified, and a power-up is conferred upon the small group of worshippers at the dolmen. It is quite possible to imagine ancient people also gathered here at this time, around their magical hovering, glowing stone, below a goddess, in the hope of abundance to come.

WALKING NOTES

There is roadside parking for Pentre Ifan at SN 10093 37014. It is then a short walk to the dolmen. Nearby Pentre-Evan Wood is a wonderful and ancient place that preserves a remnant of venerable oak forest. You can walk southeast to Craig Rhos-y-felin (SN 11668 36166) from Pentre Ifan: a distance of 2.5km (1.6 miles) with some road walking. A footpath runs alongside the Afon Brynberian to the outcrop, which is on private land, and can be viewed from the path.

The Incredible String Band:
"wise jesters" of the Preselis

43

THE DRUIDS' TEMPLE

Ersatz enchantment in a faux-Neolithic wonderland

NORTH YORKSHIRE, ENGLAND (SE 17470 78715)
OS EXPLORER 298

Britain is studded with follies, those whimsical buildings that serve little practical purpose. Follies are targeted squarely at enchanting the landscape, albeit a landscape often accessible to only a privileged few in the past. Nonetheless, the best follies retain a buzz of inspiration, radiating a weirdness lacking in our mundane modern world.

Near the brewing mecca of Masham, and just outside Ilton village, lies one of Britain's greatest follies, the Druids' Temple. The Temple is a rambling megalithic monster of trilithons, menhirs, cromlechs and altars, all the stranger for its evergreen surroundings. And although this "Shamhenge" is a newcomer to Yorkshire's ancient earth, the Temple has a powerful vibe capable of stirring even the dullest imagination.[1]

Walking through the lush, fern-scattered greenery, a pleasing cromlech is your first encounter with the faux-Neolithic before the sizeable main complex comes into view. When you enter the site proper, through an impressive trilithon entrance, you arrive in an antiquarian dreamworld – an open chamber whose internal pillars are said to represent the four elements of earth, air, fire and water. Beyond these menhirs, in what the Temple's information board dubs the "solar chamber", lies a weird megalithic dining table, screened off by an

45

enormous stone and two flankers. A little further, at the far end of the Temple, a mossy cave can be found, mysteriously termed the "Tomb of Transformation". Above the whole complex, a tall stack of slabs looms, surrounded by twelve standing stones. This deeply odd place is now of some age itself, having been visited and enjoyed for two centuries, as neatly chiselled graffiti from 1882 attests.

When the Temple was built in 1820, Druidic thinking had been resurgent in Britain for a while. William Stukeley had declared Stonehenge the work of the Druids in 1740 and would go on to describe himself as one of their number. Although little is known about ancient Druidry, a great deal was inferred and created anew when it was

"The Temple is a rambling megalithic monster of trilithons, menhirs, cromlechs and altars, all the stranger for its evergreen surroundings"

relaunched in the eighteenth century (see Midmar Stone Circle, page 130). For many, the new movement was an opportunity to imaginatively celebrate venerable traditions and to restore the reputation of the British from Roman allegations of barbarism. The Druids of the past were now viewed as far gentler folk: working in harmony with nature, they were fond of philosophy and always up for a good time. The first meeting of the Ancient Order of Druids, in 1781, was held in a London pub (the King's Arms in Soho), and when the Society of the Druids of Cardigan was established around the same time, the focus was on "literary picnics" rather than divination with entrails.[2]

It was against this potent backdrop of romantic Druidic imagery that the Druids' Temple was built. The man behind the sacred simulacrum was eccentric local landowner, William Danby. Perhaps more benevolent than many powerful men of the time, Danby opened his estate to the public and, in later life, became resolved to provide employment in the area. It was to this end that the great folly was established, Danby offering a shilling a day to those who executed his prehistoric vision.

Once the complex was built, another, even more unusual, employment opportunity was provided. Anyone prepared to live as a hermit on the site would be given food and payment in return for a seven-year stint as the Temple's very own reclusive Druid. Danby suggested the successful candidate should be willing to grow a long beard and refrain from human conversation. One plucky local appears to have lasted over four years before surrendering.

Today, the site remains a remarkable concoction and, although the builders' prowess may not rival that of the Neolithic masters, it makes for a magical encounter in the woods. In fact, it has proved a little too magical for some. In 2000, Baroness Masham of Ilton related several tales of weird goings-on at the Druids' Temple in the House of Lords. These are preserved in Hansard, the official transcript of parliamentary debates, and tell us something of the site's reputation (and that of the pressing priorities of the UK's second chamber):

A few miles from Masham, on the estate, is a realistic copy of a druid temple, with all the stones, including the sacrificial stone, in the correct positions. One Sunday afternoon, my secretary was going for a walk with a friend when she found a pig's head sitting on the altar, which gave her a terrific shock. It is thought that there has been devil worship there.

On another occasion, I had to leave home early one morning. Just outside Masham, I found a small group of Leeds University students who had spent the night at the Druids' Temple. They were cold and frightened. With the night shadows and the country noises, such as owls hooting, they had fled. As I was going towards Leeds, I gave them a lift. They told me that they had had a terrible experience.[3]

47

We found no pig's head on our visit, but can understand how those students got spooked. Even on a bright spring morning, the pine forest amplifies the smallest sounds, as we found out when a pair of esoteric ramblers began a maraca-fuelled ceremony to welcome the rising sun. Although initially startling, the percussion and accompanying incantations eventually had us bewitched. And it's easy to see why this site continues to hold such appeal despite its prosaic, and relatively recent, origins.

The folly in the woods reminds us that enchantment need not only be found in structures thousands of years old. New stories and lore can arise around relatively recent additions to the landscape. We see this in Michael Eavis's Swan Circle on the Glastonbury festival site, or even at Coul roundabout in Fife, its strange recreation of Balfarg Henge endlessly circled by people carriers and lads in hatchbacks.[4] We could do with a few more of these modern megalithic structures, not as follies but as contemporary sacred spaces. Maybe they would go some distance towards kindling reflection and reconnection in all of us.

WALKING NOTES

There is paid parking for the Druids' Temple at Swinton Bivouac (SE 17944 78721), which is part of the Swinton Estate. A café and facilities can be found here. From the car park, turn left at SE 17871 78799. It's then a short walk into the woods labelled on your OS map as Druid's Plantation to find the folly.

Down the road, Masham is the home of the legendary Theakston Brewery and its Old Peculier ale. Fine draught beers can be found at the Black Swan in Fearby, which also makes a good base for exploring the area.

WOOTTON RIVERS

An uncanny encounter with the Green Man in a magical vale

WILTSHIRE, ENGLAND (SU 19705 63242)
OS EXPLORER 157

Between Salisbury Plain and the Marlborough Downs, the Vale of Pewsey is a rambler's delight. Extending for almost twenty miles, its shire settlements trip off the tongue like a Tolkien appendix: Bottlesford, Honey Street, Huish and Clench. Here there are chalk horses and canal-side inns, prehistoric earthworks and statues of kings. The Pewsey portal is a shortcut to re-enchantment and perhaps not entered enough.

Wootton Rivers sits within this charmed region and makes a fine stop on a circular wander. The village itself is a remarkable piece of preservation, containing dozens of buildings dating to before the nineteenth century and the Tudor-era Royal Oak pub (more aptly named than most, given the village's proximity to the ancient oaks of Savernake Forest). In spring, when the leaves are beginning to unfurl and the hedgerows are shuffling into life, the parish is hard to beat.

This springtime glory is encapsulated by a character who can be found by strolling north of the village along the track appropriately known as Mud Lane. As the lane climbs towards Martinsell Hill a mysterious piece of folk art looms down from the trees. An unknown sculptor of great skill has carved a replica of the famous Green Man of Bamberg Cathedral into a living oak. Often found in churches, such "foliate heads" are surrounded

or masked by leaves, with some featuring greenery sprouting from their mouths. It is an incredible thing to come across as the natural world tumbles out of winter and into the fertility of spring all around you.

We see the Green Man right across Britain in contemporary spring parades and pageants, notably at the famous Jack in the Green festival in Hastings. However, as Keith Leech, chair of the Jack in the Green, has stated, interpreting the Green Man is "a minefield". What we do know is that the Green Man moniker was first applied to foliate heads of the kind seen in churches and cathedrals in a 1939 article by the folklorist Lady Raglan. Before that they were, well, just foliate heads. Raglan went further, throwing Robin Hood, Jack in the Green and "the King of May" into an alluring, albeit wildly imaginative, theory of the Green Man as a representation of fertility sacrifice in the mould of those described in James Frazer's influential *The Golden Bough* of 1890. There may be no historical basis for Raglan's connections, but some have been

guilty of throwing the green-faced baby out with the leafy bathwater when dismissing her claims. For although foliate heads were not linked to the idea of a Green Man before Raglan, this doesn't mean that there aren't verdant persons of varying types who pop up throughout British folk history. In fact, you could say that every age has its own Green Man, including our own.

From the Tudor period, we see "greene men" or "wyldemen" included in pageants, dressed in moss and ivy, and playfully clearing the way for the coming procession. They wore their hair long and carried impressive clubs. Pubs called the Green Man were popular from the seventeenth century, with signs showing what John Aubrey said was a

"An unknown sculptor of great skill has carved a replica of the famous Green Man of Bamberg Cathedral into a living oak"

"kind of Hercules with a green club and green leaves about his pudenda and head".[1] Around the same time, the Distiller's Company had as its coat of arms "the Green Man and Still", which featured naked and club-bearing shaggy figures. The writer John Bagford noted this was "a fit emblem for those who use that intosticating licker which berefts them of their sennes".[2] The emphasis for late medieval and early modern people was clearly on the Green Man representing the wild and uncivilised side of humanity. Interestingly, once Lady Raglan's theory became popular in the twentieth century, many Green Man pubs repainted their signs in the style of church foliate heads rather than big blokes with clubs.

In the twenty-first century, the Green Man is very much a vegetation spirit, a guardian of the natural world who strikes a particular chord with us at a time of environmental crisis. He is beloved of many contemporary pagans for precisely this reason, their traditions being committed to living in harmony with the natural world. Like nature, however, the green fellow in the woods above Wootton Rivers is inscrutable. Indeed, there is something almost unnerving about the way his eyes seem to follow you along the trail. Nonetheless, for us, the Mud Lane Green Man never ceases to confer positivity; the spirit of the season silently bearing witness in the woods, he is very much our spiritual talisman.

Past the Green Man, Mud Lane eventually brings you to Martinsell Hill, and from its summit you can see the vale spread out beneath you. No wonder it was chosen as the site of an Iron Age hillfort. In this respect, Martinsell bears more than a passing resemblance to White Horse Hill (see page 145), and also sports similar rippling folds in its geology. For ley line hunters Paul Devereux and Ian Thomson, Martinsell marked the starting point of an alignment of ancient sites that took in Avebury and the long barrow tucked away in nearby West Woods, the home of Stonehenge's sarsens (see page 231).[3] The escarpment is an imposing one in a county not known for its climbs. And as is the case with other elevated spots across the country, local lore insists that there were once community games held here, with one commentator noting that "boys used to slide down the hill on the jawbones of horses".[4]

Walking along the White Horse Trail past Martinsell, you soon arrive at Giant's Grave, the remnants of a promontory fort and a spectacular spot for a picnic. Depending on your route, the incredibly steep steps to the Giant's Grave are either ascended or descended on a circular ramble (we vote for the latter, especially on a hot day). After the descent, the path heads across vegetable fields towards the Kennet and Avon Canal and Pewsey town. In the mornings, a mist hogs the surface of the canal, mingling with the wood smoke from the barges' small hearths. Judge it right and you can arrive at lunchtime for a bite and a pint at the Waterfront pub on Pewsey Wharf. The Green Man would no doubt approve: these are the things for which springtime is made.

WALKING NOTES

There is some parking in Wootton Rivers village as well as at Martinsell Hill (SU 18347 64488) and Pewsey Wharf (SU 15787 61060). Any of these three spots can be used as a starting point for a circular walk taking in Wootton Rivers, Martinsell Hill, and Giant's Grave. The Green Man can be found on Mud Lane at SU 19837 64644. The woods adjacent to Martinsell (SU 17333 64171) are packed with bluebells in spring.

Savernake Forest lies 3km (1.9 miles) away, and is a must-visit for ancient tree fans. The many venerable specimens include the Big Belly Oak. A mere sapling at the time of the Norman Conquest and balanced precariously next to the A346, it is reputedly Britain's oldest oak. Tucked away in the woods is the sprawling mass of the King of Limbs, the tree which inspired the Radiohead album of the same name. Near a picnic area, the mighty Cathedral Oak sports a remarkable 10m (approx. 33ft) of girth and is probably second only to old Big Belly in age.

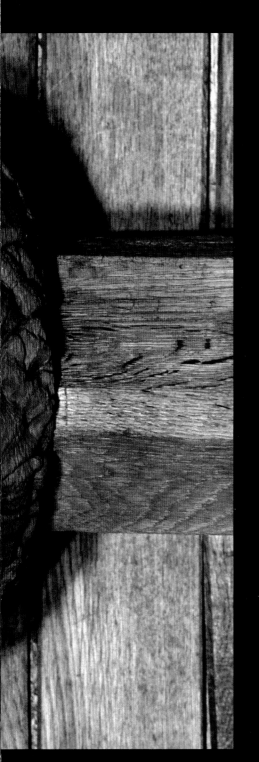

A prime example of a foliate gentleman in the parish church of St Andrew, South Tawton, Devon

BIX BOTTOM

Hauntology and history overlap in the Chiltern Hills

OXFORDSHIRE, ENGLAND (SU 72672 86977)
OS EXPLORER 171

Driving out of Henley-on-Thames, past manicured lawns, cottage gardens and quietly charging Teslas, you eventually turn onto a single-track road that winds sinuously into a valley. The hedgerows are high, and the hillsides curve gently to wooded tops. This is Bix Bottom, a portal of a place, where history and fiction overlap. For here the weird walker may travel through time, but it is also possible to set foot in an imagined past – a hauntological third dimension beyond the constraints of geography and linear history.

The valley, dotted with farmhouses and patches of mature broad-leaved woodland, is known not only for its wildlife and medieval archaeology, but for providing a key landscape within folk horror's origin story. In April 1970, filming began here on *The Blood on Satan's Claw*, a movie that would eventually take its place alongside *Witchfinder General* and *The Wicker Man* as one of the three pillars of an elusive, but enduring, idea that exposes the shadow side of Britain's rural idyll.

Directed by Piers Haggard, *The Blood on Satan's Claw* tells of the unearthing of strange remains in a field that can still be seen, ridged with furrows, in Bix Bottom today. From this haunted soil, an evil spills forth into an isolated eighteenth-century community, one that causes the village's children to form a cult with the intention of ritually assembling a demon from skin and fur grown on afflicted locals (the film is sometimes called *Satan's Skin*). The unusual tale is vividly told, and its hurriedly edited but innovative script features plenty of quotable olde worlde one-liners, most notably from the thundery Peter Wymark, who plays the sceptical judge determined to get to the bottom of all this rustic sorcery.

The real star of the film, however, is the Bix Bottom landscape, brilliantly shot by cinematographer Dick Bush. Filming on location as much as possible, and making heavy use of dark foregrounds to frame scenes, the film has an incredibly rich, naturalistic quality far

"The fictional haunted soil has seeped into the valley's reality"

removed from the campy vampire horrors that swirled around it in the early seventies.

Parking up outside St James' Church (also known as Bix Brand Old Church) puts you right at the centre of the film's most disturbing scenes. The ruined medieval building is accessed from an opening in the hedgerow and remains an eerie place. It is here that the cult's leader, Angel Blake, portrayed by Linda Hayden, sets up a demonic HQ to oversee games, ritual murder and grisly assault in the name of the fiend from the furrows. Today, the church has undergone some much-needed restoration, meaning that although it looks less like the ivy-clad ruin that was home to Angel's "godless clan", it is unlikely to disintegrate any time soon.

In late spring, the ruin is surrounded by a viridescent landscape, with wildflowers rising from the edges of the church's plot. The valley is also dotted with hawthorn blossom at this time of year, and it was while driving to the set one day that Piers Haggard was struck with the idea of blooming hawthorn branches accompanying the children of the demonic cult, most famously in the form of blossom crowns. The crowns weave further threads of meaning into the film, suggesting and subverting May queen traditions, while the bonfire at the film's climax also invokes Beltane revels, where fires symbolise purification. Indeed, the blossom crown has become something of a folk horror trope itself, the headgear being sported from Soviet chiller Viy in 1967 to the millennial weirdness of Midsommar in 2019.

St James' Church has a venerable off-screen history that is comprehensively detailed on a recently installed information board (which notably avoids any mention of the film). But this relic offers us something else, another pathway that can be trod throughout Bix Bottom. It is a door to a fictional alternate timeline, for this landscape accrues not only the genuine historical memory of the events enacted within its parameters, but transposed upon it is also the world of *Claw* writer Robert Wynne-Simmons, and the visuals conjured by Bush and Haggard. It can be seen in the witchy chalk graffiti of triangles, stars and sigils that sit alongside smileys and "Noob was here" on a restored wall of the church, waiting to be washed away in the next rainstorm. It is there in the lens through which the film nudges you to interpret the landscape: the fictional haunted soil has seeped into the valley's reality.

Walking away from the church and up towards Warburg Nature Reserve, you pass the fields where the film's ploughman, Ralph Gower, toiled, and a more recent uncanny addition to the landscape in the form of an enormous dead tree at the roadside, its grey tones incongruous in its verdant surroundings. Before you enter the nature reserve's woods, take a peek at the farm where much of the film's action takes place. Elegantly refurbished, it was up for sale at just shy of three million quid at the time of writing. Claws under floorboards and vanishing aunts as standard.

It is possible to loop back towards the church ruins through the woodland, where further scenes were shot. Ascending the valley's side between the trees, it is worth a thought about this slippery folk horror tag and how it has come to encompass not only the "unholy trinity" of *Witchfinder*, *Claw* and *Wicker Man*, but numerous other cultural expressions – from seventies public information films to the music of the Ghost Box record label and the dark satire of Richard Littler's Scarfolk universe. Perhaps the most concise framework for interpreting folk horror in film is presented by Adam Scovell in his book *Folk Horror: Hours Dreadful and Things Strange*. Here, Scovell unveils "the folk horror chain", a sequence of aspects that bind the narratives of cinematic folk horror, but with applications beyond. Scovell identifies four key elements at work. The first link in the chain is the landscape and its effect on its population. The second is isolation, often where the landscape of the chain's previous link has isolated a group of characters or a community from the wider world. The third link is that of skewed belief systems and morality which "form through this very physical but also psychical isolation".[1] Finally, the last link in the chain is the happening or summoning. Here skewed beliefs and morals connect with a violent, and sometimes supernatural, climax. While keeping spoilers at bay, *The Blood on Satan's Claw* can certainly be read within this sequence, as can the unholy trinity's other members. Walking the pathways of this landscape's fictional past allows for much rumination on the chain, and how idyllic topographies can hide or even foster malevolent forces.

Of course, the folk horror chain is more of a framework than a strict template, but it can be seen to greater or lesser degrees in all kinds of places, sometimes with the volume turned up or down on an aspect or two. It is found in several of the ghost stories of M. R. James, episodes of the black comedy *Inside No. 9,* and even gory proto-slashers such as *The Texas Chainsaw Massacre.* Beyond such frameworks of narrative interpretation, however, folk horror is probably best surmised as a vibe, that intangible quality that you just know when you see or hear it. And up here in the woods it's still at play, just as the children of Angel's tribe were, with their May crowns, bonfires and arcane rites.

WALKING NOTES

You can park in the layby outside Bix Brand Old Church (su 72672 86977), and there are further options in Warburg Nature Reserve. Just carry on up the same road. Bix Bottom is crossed by many footpaths, including the Oxfordshire Way and Chiltern Way, so there is plenty of scope for mapping a great ramble. A simple loop can be achieved from the church by walking up past Pages Farm (su 72055 87763) and climbing through the wood to Lodge Farm (su 72303 88228). You can then drop down through Freedom Wood and back to the church. The seventeenth-century Rainbow Inn in Middle Assendon is the nearest pub. A range of walks have been plotted from here, with details on the Rainbow Inn website.

TIGH NAM BODACH

Animist ritual practice in a remote Scottish glen

PERTH AND KINROSS, SCOTLAND (NN 38053 42711)
OS EXPLORER OL48

Tigh nam Bodach is one of Britain's most enigmatic and isolated ritual sites. This simple pagan shrine sits below snow-capped peaks in a side valley of the mighty Glen Lyon, the longest enclosed glen in Scotland and, according to Sir Walter Scott, the "loneliest and loveliest" too. Outside a modest yet beautifully constructed shelter sits a family of Gaelic myth, headed by a mysterious goddess, the Cailleach. The goddess, her husband (the Bodach of the shrine's name) and their children are all represented by strangely humanoid stones, which have been shaped over millennia by the fast-flowing Allt na Cailliche stream. At Beltane, on 1 May, locals take the stone family from their house to watch over the land and ensure its fertility, ritually returning them inside on Samhain, 1 November. In late spring, it is a marvellous thing to walk through Glen Lyon to witness the figures enjoying the view over their glen.

The journey to Tigh nam Bodach often begins by driving some 16km (10 miles) down a single-track road through stunning scenery to Lubreoch Dam at the western end of Glen Lyon. The road runs out at the enormous dam, which holds Loch Lyon at bay in the name of hydroelectricity. From here, a rough track climbs around the loch through a towering landscape of mountains and waterfalls for around

10km (6 miles) to the shrine. It is not uncommon for the whole route to be completely devoid of people, bar the occasional wild camper, enjoying the freedoms denied to hikers south of the border in England, where the right to roam is outlawed via anachronistic nineteenth-century laws.

This is grand rambling country, and the glen encourages you to take your time. The great chronicler of life in Glen Lyon, Alexandra Stewart, recalls her father treading these paths, and the deep connection of local people to the land. For him, "this walk would be alive with the lore and legend of nearly two thousand years," she notes. And like her father, Stewart walked actively in this place, a place where "there was always something to watch, some association to remember".[1]

Stewart's father would not recognise parts of Glen Lyon today, particularly Loch Lyon, which grew dramatically with the creation of the dam. In its eastern section, near the dam itself, the loch has an unusually industrial aspect; the many waterfalls that tumble down from on high are occasionally directed by steel outflow pipes beneath the track. Some that have outlived their usefulness lie prone and shattered below, like the rusted cocoons of gigantic metal moths. Even in a landscape such as this, modernity is impossible to escape.

Thankfully, no structures other than a handy wooden bridge interfere with the magnificent Eos Eoghannan waterfall that soon crosses your path, its deep ravine populated with rowan and birch. This is the kind of place that, if it were more accessible, would no doubt be thronged at this time of year. However, it is the secluded nature of this landscape that makes it the perfect spot for the Cailleach. Running through modern Scottish and Irish mythology, the legend of the Cailleach may well have begun life in literature before tumbling into the world of folklore.[2] The goddess is a shaper of mountains and wild places, a bringer of storms and winter. She is often seen as a fearsome figure, but in Glen Lyon she reveals a more benevolent aspect, as can be seen in Tigh nam Bodach's origin story.

One version of the tale begins when a giant man and woman are seen in the remotest part of the glen during a terrible blizzard. Local people shelter the pair, providing what accommodation they can for such unusually large visitors while they wait out the storm. A bond soon forms between the giants and their hosts, and the couple settle down in Glen Lyon, once a large enough dwelling can be built. It is here that the woman gives birth to a daughter. This is a happy time: the days are warm, the animals are healthy and quarrels are few. Eventually, however, the family tell the people that they have to leave. Their parting gift to those who made them so welcome is the promise of a plentiful and trouble-free existence in the upper glen. All they ask is that they will be remembered.[3]

"The stones themselves seem genuinely imbued with life, appearing at once vulnerable and impervious to the whims of time"

The story goes on to note that, as a result of this promise, stones were chosen to represent the Cailleach, the Bodach and their daughter, Nighean, and a small house was built in the style of their original dwelling. The ritual of sheltering and removing the stones was then begun by the people of the glen. Although it is unclear how old the animistic practices associated with Tigh nam Bodach actually are (some say they were developed in the eighteenth or nineteenth centuries by shepherds), the place names in this landscape certainly suggest a venerable association with the goddess.

Turning away from the loch, the track leads you up towards even more impressive mountains, speckled with snow. Here there are streams to cross that can feel more like rivers following a downpour. After the stepping stone crossing of Allt Meurain stream, you climb into Glen Cailliche. This is very much the goddess' territory, with the powerful Allt na Cailliche running alongside the track. When the shrine is finally spied, it is hard not to run over the marshy ground in excitement, greeting (but not handling, of course) the sacred stones like old friends. The family's modest home is modelled on a shieling, the simple house once used by farmers in the summer months up in the glens. Not long ago it underwent a complete rebuild in traditional fashion, incorporating a 300-year-old oak plank below its characteristic turf roof. Its recent overhaul fits perfectly within this place of water, stone and sky.

Sitting in front of Tigh nam Bodach in the welcome warmth of a late spring day is a moving experience. The stones themselves seem genuinely imbued with life, appearing at once vulnerable and impervious to the whims of time. Pilgrims have left items around the shrine – a wooden star, a ram's horn, a piece of shining quartz. Few sites tell of our connection to the seasons and the land like this. In its simple, localised ritual practice, Tigh nam Bodach encapsulates an ancient relationship. The Celtic scholar Anne Ross noted that when the land was flooded, extending the loch for the new dam, there were fewer folk to carry out the ritual. Happily, it has been maintained by Glen Lyon's shepherds, and, if anything, attachment to the custom has grown even stronger in these parts.[4] When further hydroelectric works threatened to encroach upon the Cailleach's hidden glen, the plans were soon nixed by concerned locals and academics. Here, the stones still matter.

WALKING NOTES

The simplest way to access the site is to find a spot to park at Lubreoch Dam (NN 45932 41892). You can then walk around Loch Lyon and up to Tigh nam Bodach (NN 38053 42711) which is around 10km (6 miles) away. There are streams to cross, so waterproof footwear is a must. This is a remote one – there's no phone signal and, being subject to the vicissitudes of the Scottish weather, the right gear is essential. Make sure you have a route mapped and take a pal.

Situated at the opposite end of Glen Lyon to Tigh nam Bodach is the village of Fortingall (a fifty-minute drive from Lubreoch Dam), a small place with a hefty mythic pedigree. Fortingall is home to a famous ancient yew tree (some parking at NN 74156 47011), which is thought to be between 2,000 and 3,000 years old. The remnants of three stone circles lie at the eastern edge of the village, close to the River Lyon. Another monument, Càrn na Marbh or "the cairn of the dead", began life as a Bronze Age burial mound before it was opened in the fourteenth century to hold the bodies of Fortingall's plague victims. Further antiquities can be seen in the church, including a Celtic handbell and fragments of Pictish stones.

PADSTOW

An iconic community bonding ceremony in a picturesque fishing port

CORNWALL (SW 92013 75346)
OS EXPLORER 106

May Day in Padstow is iconic for a reason. The arcane, multilayered and visually arresting folk tradition of the 'Obby 'Oss festival has long intrigued outsiders, while the people of this town (every single one of them it seems) are fiercely protective of their rite. This revenant speaks of community, heritage, Cornish identity and pride, and perhaps most importantly, of the coming of the sun.

The festivities begin in Padstow on May Eve, a time traditionally fraught with superstitious meaning, once even more so than Halloween. Mirroring that autumnal festival, 30 April was thought to be the preserve of fairies and goblins, who roamed the countryside, while fires were set and, indeed, leaped in an echo of the ancient rites of Beltane.[1] Winter was finally sent on its way and the summer's warmth was nigh.

It is also on May Eve that the 'Oss, a unique interpretation of the classic English hobby horse, wakes from its slumber. Outside the Golden Lion pub, the "Night Song" is lustily sung, and out slips the Old 'Oss from its stable. Its sleek black form dips away from the crowd, the bold red of its facial features flashing in the darkness. The beast will return on the rising of the sun.

75

"The 'Obby 'Oss festival is a conduit for reconnection to the concerns of our ancestors. Through the rite, a community is bound together and a season is greeted with open arms"

In the days preceding the festival, before the "Night Song" is even sung, Padstow's transformation begins. The atmosphere heightens and there is a subtle shift in vibration. This quintessential Cornish fishing harbour is repurposed as a ritual space for celebrating the returning spring. Padstonians nowadays bring in the May on 4x4s and pickup trucks piled high with freshly cut branches, the streets and houses soon bedecked in their costume of flags and leafy boughs. At the centre of it all is the giant maypole.

On May morning, two 'Osses are soon out and about, the Blue Ribbon 'Oss (a post-First World War addition) joining the Old 'Oss for the fun and games. Each creature comes complete with a "teaser" who brandishes a painted club and leads the 'Oss in its merry dance. All through the proceedings, the "Day Song" is sung by the processing crowds, accompanied by drums and accordions. The folk are decked in white clothes, set off with colours showing their allegiance – red for the Old 'Oss and blue for its more recently introduced cousin. The "Day Song" is incessant: it has an ineffably woozy quality that reverberates through the streets, echoing the ghosts of Padstonian ancestors and seemingly capable of opening a portal to some bygone age through force of repetition. The past and the present harmonised, the townspeople dipping and swaying to the music in their idiosyncratic skank, the 'Oss is afoot, summer is afoot.

The song's enigmatic lyrical content is soon fixed in the memory of all attendees, not least a curious lament for St George, during which the music slows and the dancers appear to comfort the 'Oss:

O! where is St George,
O!, where is he O,
He is out in his long boat on the salt sea O.

Then, with a cry of "Oss! Oss! Wee Oss!" the beast is reinvigorated and resumes its duties. With such death and resurrection themes, and the propensity for the 'Oss to capture young maidens beneath

its skirts (married within the year they used to say), Padstow's May Day celebrations were rich pickings for early folklorists fixated on Victorian theories of ancient fertility rituals. And even though scholars now date the tradition to the late eighteenth century rather than the distant pagan past, it does, undeniably, speak to a deep thread woven into our psyche – the welcoming of summer, of life and, yes, fertility.[2] In this way, the 'Obby 'Oss festival is a conduit for reconnection to the concerns of our ancestors. Through the rite, a community is bound together and a season is greeted with open arms. Its insular positivity and unique format is unlike any other custom in the land, a fact that has no doubt ensured its survival when other traditions have faded. As they sing:

> *Unite and unite and let us all unite,*
> *For summer is a-come unto day,*
> *And whither we are going we will all unite,*
> *In the merry morning of May.*

WALKING NOTES

There is a park and ride option for Padstow as you enter the town on the A389. Although the place is obviously busy on May Day, plan ahead and you should be fine. Roads in the town itself are closed during the celebrations. If you fancy a ramble, the Camel Trail begins in Padstow and can be followed to Bodmin and on to Wenfordbridge. Tracing the route of former railway lines, you can hit the trail on foot, bike or even horse.

Above the town, you will find Padstow Cemetery (sw 90970 75267), the resting place of Edward Woodward, aka *The Wicker Man*'s Sergeant Howie. There is something wonderful and strange about the actor being at rest here, while "For summer is a-come unto day" resounds and the 'Oss cuts capers in the streets below.

COOPER'S HILL

A chaotic springtime custom tumbles down a Cotswold hillside

GLOUCESTERSHIRE, ENGLAND (SO 89212 14706)
OS EXPLORER 179

In the final days of spring, a centuries-old custom is performed in the Gloucestershire parish of Brockworth. This is, however, no sedate tea and biscuits affair; the Cooper's Hill Cheese Roll has a DIY outlaw energy more akin to a rave or free festival. This is folk tradition as an extreme sport. The pluckiest villagers leg it down the devastating slope of Cooper's Hill following a nine-pound wheel of Double Gloucester cheese, with the intention of being the first to cross the finish line at the bottom. The winner takes the cheese, of course, and there are no prizes for second place, but if you find yourself at the foot of the hill still able to walk, that too is considered a victory.

The Cheese Roll is a relic of a larger "wake" (parish festival) that was traditionally held on top of Cooper's Hill, and involved all kinds of wonderful weirdness, from shin kicking to smock races and gurning.[1] While examples elsewhere died out (see White Horse Hill, page 145), the cheese-rolling element of the wake has been kept alive by Brockworth locals since the early nineteenth century at least. Immortalised in a recent Netflix documentary and countless "and finally" news pieces, Gloucestershire's most charming health and safety nightmare now attracts competitors from across the world. And yet, this remains a brilliantly weird parish custom with a determinedly independent spirit, requiring remarkable physical commitment from participants. As Cotswold lad Charlie Cooper noted in the fifth issue of *Weird Walk*, "It's staggering what people put their bodies through for a fairly modest-sized wheel of cheese."

The day often begins with a breakfast at the Toby Carvery in Brockworth. Here, there's a pre-match, anticipatory vibe among the industrial vats of bacon and early-bird Yorkshire puds. The excitement is palpable as spectators reminisce about cheese races past, and contestants swap tips for the coming descent. You might even spot Brockworth legend and winner of twenty-plus races, Chris Anderson, sitting alongside the cheeses themselves: a bit like having breakfast next to Messi with the Champions League trophy on his table.

Full English duly devoured, it's time to swap the bright lights of the fruit machines for the peerless Cotswold countryside, and the journey up to Cooper's Hill. Once you swing a left off the road and begin your ramble, the idyll levels crank up substantially. Ahead, the

"In the modern world below, red tape and risk assessments hold sway; on top of Cooper's Hill, however, there are no such fusspot concerns. People just know that in late spring you fling yourself down a hill after a cheese in these parts"

rolling countryside is dotted with small, sun-dappled woods, while the hedgerow alongside the path ripples gently with birdsong. In late spring, this is a particularly enchanting stroll. And if the route soon becomes more taxing as you ascend the first hill, it's worth noting that this isn't where the cheeses will roll: this is the pre-hill. It's only after a further hike through the trees that you sight the main event. Cooper's Hill is a crazy incline, sprouting out of an already impressive hillscape. Running for over 180m (200yd), it is so steep as to be concave in sections. From the bottom, it is hard to ever imagine anyone running down it. But they do.

Although the police close local roads, and stern posters warn the crowd of the potential for injury, the event isn't deemed "official", so it has been administered and controlled by the villagers themselves for some time, without a central organiser. Whenever moves are made to halt the custom due to safety concerns, it takes place anyway. In the modern world below, red tape and risk assessments hold sway; on top of Cooper's Hill, however, there are no such fusspot concerns. People just know that in late spring you fling yourself down a hill after a cheese in these parts. And it's this spontaneous and excitable feel that adds so much to the event: long before the first races at midday, there is a buzz about the hill.

After some howling feedback, the improvised PA is ready to facilitate announcements, interviews and, somewhat weirdly, a northern soul DJ set. Fans of juxtaposition will enjoy moving to Sly and the Family Stone while the white-coated master of cheese rolling ceremonies poses for photos in full traditional regalia, carrying his Double Gloucester. Soon, spectators crowd the sides and base of the hill, while some (including the competitors) hug the summit. Well-prepared onlookers have lugged carrier bags of cider and lager up the slope and there are plenty of cans on the go as race time approaches and the runners limber up. Hair of the dog and Dutch courage are in plentiful supply. The village die-hards, the international contingent, and a few bedraggled souls who somehow fancy it after pulling an all-nighter, are getting their game faces on.

There are three men's races, one women's race and an uphill race for the kids. And they are all a sight to behold. For the downhill main

events the crowd begins a slow rumbling chant of "cheese, cheese" before the dairy is unleashed and the tumbling, stumbling runners head to the bottom. Some attempt a nimble navigation of the hill's various channels and ruts; others just seem to spin uncontrollably. Imagine an ill-fated infantry charge "over the top" on a First World War battlefield but tilted ninety degrees. Nearly all are eventually scooped up by the rugby team, tasked with preventing competitors from smashing into the fence at the bottom. It's completely brilliant madness.

The Cheese Roll is not a tradition preserved in aspic by the authenticity police; it continues to evolve while retaining its key components. In its good-natured abandon, it demonstrates both a defiant community spirit and an inclusive welcome. It is notable that up on Cooper's Hill we saw a diversity more akin to modern Britain than at many other customs. The old ways are for everyone, and risking your neck for a wheel of cheese seems to be one way of transcending boundaries and bringing folk together.

WALKING NOTES

On the day of the Cheese Roll, you can park at the Toby Carvery in Brockworth all day for a fee. From here, you can take a left at SO 89795 15947 to begin a slightly longer, off-road journey up to Cooper's Hill. Pass through the woods at SO 89551 15123 and you will soon come to the base of the hill, near a small group of houses and with impressive views over Gloucestershire.

The whole area is worth exploring. Cooper's Hill sits right on the Cotswold Way if you fancy incorporating a section of this trail into your visit. Down the road lies the village of Painswick (9km/5.6 miles from Brockworth), reputedly one of the most haunted spots in England, while Great Witcombe Roman Villa is tucked away nearby, just off the Cotswold Way (SO 90150 14325).

SUMMER

Summer has always been a high time. The season opened its arms to our ancestors, as it does to us: longer and warmer days allow for play as well as work, pleasures intensified by an inviting outdoor world.

Dances such as those enacted today at Thaxted would have once been immensely popular, while festivities, such as the folkloric open-air wedding at Stanton Drew or the ancient tradition of the scouring of the Uffington White Horse, could take advantage of the (occasionally) balmy weather. Gentle breezes may rustle through the crop fields as a reminder of the harvest that lies ahead, but now is the moment to make merry in the sun.

Midsummer is a particularly powerful occasion, the very peak of the wheel of the year. It is one best observed, in our opinion, within an ancient circle of stones. Avebury is our circle of choice, that mind-bending village of juxtaposition and a place seemingly existing in multiple time periods simultaneously. Other sites, such as Bryn Celli Ddu on

Anglesey, betray a reverence for midsummer in their design, and are places of heightened potency when visited at this point of the year. Castlerigg in Cumbria may be thronged with tourists in summer, but an early start allows you to revel in the grandest of Neolithic settings in all its seasonal glory, a location that demonstrates more than any other the ancients' flair for picking their spot to build.

Summer is a fine season for rambling in general, of course, when stunning landscapes like that of Bodmin Moor can be explored thoroughly on foot, taking in numerous fascinating monuments in an area that spins a narrative web from its haunted soil. Or perhaps it is the time for a tour of Aberdeenshire's peerless recumbent stone circles, of which Midmar is a prime example, and another site where history is rendered as a palimpsest. Wherever you are on these islands, the promise of summers past, present and future is only a stroll away.

SELECTED SUMMER OBSERVANCES:
· Lanark Lanimers Week – early June
· Great Knaresborough Bed Race – second Saturday in June
· Abingdon Mayor of Ock Street – Saturday nearest 19 June
· Whalton Baal Fire – 4 July
· Berwick Curfew Run – Wednesday in July
· Grasmere Rushbearing – Saturday in mid-July
· River Thames Swan Upping – third week in July
· National Eisteddfod of Wales – first week in August
· Burryman's Parade in South Queensferry – second Friday
  in August

STANTON DREW

An idyllic Somerset village resonates with megalithic folklore

SOMERSET, ENGLAND (ST 59950 63246)
OS EXPLORER 155

The village of Stanton Drew in Somerset is that perfect kind of English settlement, with a rare but potent blend of folklore, farmsteads, an old toll house that looks exactly like a mushroom, and a massive ritual complex of stone circles. It practically vibrates with stored-up mythic energy. It is also a site intimately connected with music, for according to the famous legend the monuments here are the scene of a substantial (and blasphemous) historic rave – a petrified mid-banger snapshot, frozen in time by the Devil himself. This tale has generated a sonic momentum of its own, embedding itself in compositions across generations. Sift through the layers, however, and there may be even older and deeper musicality at work among the megaliths.

Of all the stories that have grown up around standing stones, that of the petrified dancers is one of the most persistent. The wedding at Stanton Drew is an oft-repeated incarnation of this tale and, like its narrative siblings in Cornwall and Devon, it's very much cautionary, a warning against excessive revelry – the dangerous hedonism of dancing! – and the breaking of social conventions of the kind reinforced by the post-Reformation Church.

The story opens on a bright summer Saturday long ago, when a wedding party assembled in the village. The bride and groom had hired the finest fiddler in Somerset to play the feast – his music was wondrous, and its powers hard

93

to resist. Beginning with simple country tunes, his playing grew more and more febrile as the sun sank and the booze flowed.

It was some hours before the parson moved away from the crowd and whispered in the fiddler's ear that it would be unwise to continue the dances past midnight and into the Sabbath. The fiddler, a pious man, agreed and set aside his bow. However, seeing their musician move to collect his pay, the bride and groom became enraged. The bride, somewhat worse for drink, declared, "This dance will persist even if hell must provide the fiddler!"

Ill-chosen words for sure. From the centre of the crowd, a tall man appeared, dressed in red. He held a fiddle and soon began to play. If the guests willingly surrendered to the tunes of the evening's opening act, then this new headliner's playing was very different. This was a set for the ages. His music accelerated in such a way that the dancers became a blur of motion. Thoughts of the Sabbath disappeared from their minds; there was only the music and the moment, an ecstatic frenzy, a constant pulse of energy that eventually, upon the rising of the sun, shivered and stuck. Some comedown. The tune that rang out across the county of Somerset that night has long since faded, but the guests remain, as the stones of Stanton Drew.

The wedding story was well known to the seventeenth-century antiquary John Aubrey, who played happily among the stones as a child and returned many years later to find the circles in disrepair. "The stones have been diminishing fast these past few years", he wrote anxiously. "I must stop this if I can."[1] Today, although much has been lost, the village's antiquities remain remarkable. However, for such an important location, Stanton Drew is decidedly unpretentious, thankfully lacking the paternalist oversight of other sites its equal. There is very little mediation between you and the history. This is a place of handmade signs and honesty boxes rather than interactive video walls and National Trust fleeces. One of the most ancient parts of the complex, the cove, sits in the beer garden of the local pub, the Druid's Arms. The three unusually shaped stones that make up the cove (three megaliths forming an open box) play their own part in the wedding tale, becoming the parson, the bride and the bridegroom, in the words of William Stukeley, "thus petrify'd".[2]

The Druid's Arms sits at an intersection where millennia of evolving ritual behaviour in Stanton Drew can be observed at once. The beer garden

North Somerset legend, Adge Cutler

perches at a vantage point where the land rises behind the pub, and wooden benches and Stella Artois umbrellas vie for floor space with the three imposing megaliths of the cove. Two stones stand upright, with a large, flat recumbent looking for all the world like some kind of altar. Stukeley's 1723 drawing of the cove shows all three standing, so visions of be-cloaked moonlit sacrifices (before that date) must be banished for now. While taking refreshments it is worth positioning yourself towards the far corner railings of the garden and enjoying the forced perspective of the stones matching in height – and even exceeding, with some careful crouching and craning of the neck – the thirteenth-century church tower rising beyond the thick blanket of ivy that tops the boundary wall. The pagan and Christian ritual spaces of this Somerset village, separated by thousands of years, superimposed over a bowl of chips and a glass of scrumpy. Here you have rural modernity quietly harmonising with its pagan history and lore; the past in the present is a year-round ritual here at Stanton Drew.

"stones stood tall in a beer garden, like ancient regulars cradling pints and crafty ciggies"

The church, the great circles and the continuance of modern village life overlap in that pleasingly incongruent way that deep history has a habit of creating. The temporal disruption of stone circles in a field nestled in the gentle green swoop of the Chew Valley is one thing, but stones stood tall in a beer garden, like ancient regulars cradling pints and crafty ciggies, is something else altogether. It would be unwise not to consult with these sentinels of the tavern – they have seen it all. The levels of incongruence, and in our view, enchantment, that this creates ramp up markedly. The Druid's Arms at Stanton Drew is a place to revel in uncanny juxtaposition.

The story of Stanton Drew's famous wedding would come to have a strange folk revival afterlife when the tale was written up as "The Dancers of Stanton Drew" by the enterprising lyricist and 1950s children's author Muriel Holland. With its combination of mysterious stones, rustic disobedience and a particularly insistent devil ("Stop! cried the dancers, No! cried the fiddler, He kept on in spite of all their moans") the song was soon in the repertoire of many folk groups, most notably Dorset's finest, the Yetties (proud bell-jangling members of the Wessex Morris Men when not in the recording studio), who included the track on their boozy 1971 LP, *Our Friends the Yetties*.

Chief Wurzel Adge Cutler would also reach for Stanton Drew when he was penning his take on the consequences of European economic integration and searching for a perfectly incongruous rural spot. The provincial lyrics of "When the Common Market Comes to Stanton Drew" have often been read as defiantly Eurosceptic, but that does Adge's deft satirical humour a disservice as he comments on public opinion ("The papers say so, so I s'pose 'tis true") and generally sounds pretty chuffed with the prospect of continental culture arriving in Somerset ("the Druid's Arms won't close till ver' nigh two!").

Nevertheless, local MP and self-styled temporal anomaly Jacob Rees-Mogg would still nod to the track when delivering an address in front of the stones during a moment of 2019 general election weirdness.

It's not only wannabe aristocratic eccentrics that have made musical pilgrimages to Stanton Drew of late, however. The avant-pastoral record label Folklore Tapes visited the site to imbibe the vibes and create the inaugural entry in a proposed *Megalithic Monuments* series of recordings. David Chatton Barker and Ian Humberstone have used their label to dive deep into British lore, and that of the West Country in particular; and on *Stanton Drew Stone Circle* they set a Victorian retelling of the petrified wedding alongside uncanny manipulations of stringed instruments and delayed analogue apparitions. The collection wouldn't feel out of place as the soundtrack for a Nigel Kneale TV play set amid the stones, something indicated by the titling of tracks such as "Stone Tape Movement I".

Stanton Drew also appears within the bucolic reveries conjured by the duo known as Peter Talisman, whose collision of folk guitar and stuttering, melodic electronica debuted on 2021's *Lord of the Harvest*, and which features the wonderfully named "The Absolute Scene at Stanton Drew". In an online game that accompanies the release and nods to the project's folk horror vibe, players explore a swaying cornfield, uncovering menhirs in a strange parallel to John Aubrey's return to the crop-filled circles of Stanton Drew as an adult: "The corn was ripe and ready for harvest at this time of year, so I could not measure the stones properly as I wished."[3]

Curiously, it is possible that these modern musical interpretations build on ancient acoustic foundations within the complex itself. Although Stanton Drew is a relatively quiet site compared to the likes of road-ravaged Stonehenge, the modern world is certainly audible, be it from distant traffic, agricultural machinery or the occasional ringtone. Indeed, it is difficult for us to imagine how heightened a Neolithic sense of hearing would have been; the rush of a river, the howl of a wolf or the laughter of friends would never have been coloured by the hum of the industrial world. This awareness doubtless meant that sound was incredibly important culturally. As the pioneer of archaeoacoustics Paul Devereux stated, "It is inconceivable that ancient people would have selected a cave or built a monument in which the acoustics were not absolutely right for whatever ritual activity was to be carried out there."[4]

Devereux notes that the coves of Avebury and Stanton Drew featured particularly powerful acoustic capabilities. The positioning of stones as a cove means they can amplify some sound sources while filtering out others. A sacred rite that relied on musical performance with an audience of celebrants would have been ideal here, and the desired focusing of sound may have been a key design consideration. Although, like the music of the fiddler at Stanton Drew's wedding, the soundtrack of such observances is lost, a simple clap of the hands or a call within a prehistoric site can reveal some of its sonic potential.

Of course, the perfect time for celebration, for music and dance, is high summer, as the petrified wedding guests know only too well. For the ancients, this was also a time of festival, perhaps when the spiritual and acoustic properties of the stones were at their peak. And this is the perfect time to visit today, to wander the circles and the cove. For when the sun rises over Stanton Drew, the old stories, and the old sounds, seem just as alive as ever.

WALKING NOTES

There is parking near the church. From here you can visit the Druid's Arms and the cove in its beer garden. The homemade Druid's pie (beef in a beer sauce) is recommended. The stone circles begin at ST 59950 63246 and can be accessed from a pathway at ST 59823 63266. Pop a quid in the honesty box as you go by.

While you are in the area, the wonderful Stoney Littleton Long Barrow is well worth a visit (ST 73500 57199). Some 22km (13.7 miles) from Stanton Drew, this 30m (98ft) barrow can be entered with plenty of ducking. A beautiful ammonite fossil can be seen on the stone slab at the entrance to the tomb.

THAXTED

An annual recharging of the irrepressible folk-dance spirit

ESSEX, ENGLAND (TL 61141 30954)
OS EXPLORER 195

Thaxted in Essex is a bona fide morris-dancing mecca. Here, on the first weekend of June, the Morris Ring organises a celebration of folk dance that brings sides from across the country to the picturesque rural town. It was in Thaxted that the Morris Ring was founded, and the tradition runs deep in these parts. The annual assembly serves as a powerful bonding ritual for the morris community. For one weekend each year, the half-timbered buildings of Thaxted reverberate with the reedy drone of accordions and the clacking of willow sticks as the collective folk dance battery is fully recharged.

The Ring was once a bastion of all-male dancing, but times have changed, and with inspirational female sides such as Boss Morris leading the way, exclusionary practices now seem limited to the morris margins. At Thaxted these days, you'll see mixed as well as all-female sides in among the action. But although the Thaxted Morris Weekend is a folk custom must-see, this place is perfect for a wander anyway, with much to offer the weird walker even when the hankies and bells are safely put away.

Morris emerged from a courtly dance craze that made the leap from the nobility to the ordinary people of England in the late Middle Ages. In the hands of the common folk, the dance enjoyed a love–hate relationship with authority, being seen on the one hand as a useful church fundraiser,

103

"For one weekend each year, the half-timbered buildings of Thaxted reverberate with the reedy drone of accordions and the clacking of willow sticks as the collective folk dance battery is fully recharged"

and on the other as being possessed of an ungodly, anarchic spirit. Puritans were particularly agitated by the working person's morris, with the first literary mention of the dance in England being a 1582 text by Christopher Fetherston titled *A Dialogue Agaynst Light, Lewde and Lascivious Dauncing*, wherein the author takes aim at people enjoying May Games. Fetherston had obviously heard of a particularly interesting form of morris as he comments, "it hath been toulde that your morice dauncers have daunced naked in nettes: what greater entisement unto naughtines could have been devised?" Naughtiness indeed.[1] The same puritanical attitude was applied to other aspects of spring and summer celebrations, although people were keen to keep their traditions running. Indeed, when the Long Parliament finally outlawed maypoles in 1644, the dancing didn't end but was driven underground. Historian Ronald Hutton has drawn parallels between illicit maypole dancing and 1990s rave culture, with young people introducing portable maypoles and local enforcers given deliberately misleading tip-offs as to where dances would be held.[2]

Over the next few hundred years, morris dancing itself underwent several declines and resurgences, developing distinct local characteristics, before being established in the revived form that we know today in the first half of the twentieth century. And Thaxted would play a major role in this revival, its morris men being the oldest revival side in the country, and the town hosting its annual festival since 1927 (a consecutive record broken only by the COVID-19 pandemic).

Approaching Thaxted, its decorative town sign announces its folk dance status with a couple of prominent morris men supporting an emblem of crossed swords. The real dancers tour the pubs of local villages in groups over the weekend, roving amiably with pewter tankards at the ready in between performances. On Saturday afternoon, the town begins to broil with morris as the various tours return to base and flowery hats and sashes abound in the summer sun. Beasts and hobby horses jostle with fools in jester's gear, and old friends catch sight of each other, clocking some familiar colours. While the atmosphere builds, a stroll out to Thaxted's windmill allows you to take in the medieval three-storied buildings and cobbled road near the surprisingly large and beautiful parish church. The frequent low rumble of planes on their Stansted flightpaths is the only jolt to the twenty-first century.

By the time you return to town, much ale has been drunk in the three pubs, especially the suitably named Maypole, where dancers seem to outnumber punters. Serious business lies ahead, however, and it is a wonderful thing to see the sides assemble as the church clock nears six. Eventually, they process in a neat pincer movement down to Town Street, now closed to traffic and thronged with people. The musicians lead the procession, their tunes echoing down towards the ancient guildhall, while steps are danced, hankies waved and bells jangled. Once settled in the main thoroughfare, massed dancing commences before each side showcases their own performance, flamboyantly introduced over a portable PA. The evening culminates in a haunting rendition of the iconic Abbots Bromley Horn Dance (see page 164) by Thaxted Morris, a peak pagan moment – deep Staffordshire vibes transported to the heart of Essex.

Although morris dancing has often been performed at different times of the year throughout its history, there is certainly something about its movements and rhythms that speak to the warmer seasons. It is such a joyful form of expression, and a profoundly community-minded one, that it makes sense that out here in Town Street there are folk from many different backgrounds with kids on their shoulders and pints in hand, soaking up the positive energy. Because that is what does emanate from this strange, peculiarly British dance – an energy, and an optimism, which connects to the old ways but knows that customs also evolve.

WALKING NOTES

Thaxted is surprisingly well served for parking, with a few free car parks. If you arrive a little ahead of the dancing on the Morris Weekend, you should be able to find a spot. The town is also connected by a bus, which passes through on its way to Saffron Walden.

Main attractions include the famous guildhall (TL 61141 30954) and windmill (TL 60963 30829). Thaxted's church (TL 61048 31023) is one of the largest in Essex and usually features a display charting the history of morris in Thaxted during the weekender. Opposite the church, the Swan Hotel hosts the dancers prior to their Saturday perambulation and serves top-notch pints and food. Walk past the Swan and on to Newbiggen Street to see the plaque commemorating the founding of the Morris Ring on this spot – now number 32 Newbiggen Street.

CASTLERIGG

The ultimate union of monumental landscape and perfect stone circle

CUMBRIA, ENGLAND (NY 29145 23634)
OS EXPLORER OL04

The Lake District is particularly rich with megalithic monuments, but few sites compare to the grandeur of Castlerigg. This stone circle has been route one to re-enchantment for centuries, with Romantic poets such as Keats and Coleridge yomping around its ancient perimeter and replenishing their creative muse at the magic circle above Keswick. Ann Radcliffe, author of the Gothic masterpiece *The Mysteries of Udolpho*, was particularly smitten on her visit. Radcliffe was not only a great writer, but a pioneering eighteenth-century rambler with an eye for uncanny landscapes. At Castlerigg, she noted that the "seclusion and sublimity were, indeed, well suited to the deep and wild mysteries of the Druids".[1]

Radcliffe was right, of course. This is as magnificent a setting for a stone circle as you are ever likely to encounter – a fact that is not lost on the thousands of tourists who stop off here each year during a visit to Cumbria. To witness this place at the crack of dawn in midsummer, however – a time when there are relatively few visitors – allows for maximum drama. Mountains, sky and standing stones combine to giddying effect at this megalithic cathedral in the Lakes. The old stone engineers' real estate selection rarely disappoints, but at Castlerigg it reaches its zenith.

"This is as magnificent a setting for a stone circle as you are ever likely to encounter"

The circle itself is early, dating to the Neolithic, and remarkably well preserved for such a relatively accessible site. Thirty-eight stones remain here from an original forty-two. Unusually, some of the stones form a rectangular section which nudges itself into the (slightly egg-shaped) circle to form an internal enclosure. It is the power of the monument's relationship with its landscape, however, which causes sharp intakes of breath when waiting for the first signs of the summer sun. This is one of those thin places, where at certain moments the veil between the temporal and the eternal is apt to lift. Cloud banks unfurl and retreat, the weather ever-changeable here even in summer. You are surrounded by mighty peaks whose names, as the author Andrew Michael Hurley points out in the third issue of *Weird Walk*, run like a magical incantation: Helvellyn, Blencathra, Skiddaw and Grisedale. Sightings of a spectral cohort of mounted soldiers in the direction of Blencathra have been recorded by folklorists down the ages; there can be few backdrops better suited to such an eerie procession.

In the Neolithic, this part of the world was famed for its axes. Three local examples were excavated at Castlerigg, possibly deposited ritually during the Late Neolithic, and some have suggested that the circle may have played a role in the prehistoric axe trade, perhaps as a ceremonial meeting point. These were axes quarried and fashioned from the rock of the Langdale Pikes, notably the imposing Pike of Stickle, fell walker Alfred Wainwright's "steep ladder to heaven". Such a fell would have seemed even more otherworldly in the ancient past, imbuing its geology with a mysterious power. Axes wrought from Langdale's

distinctive blue-green volcanic rock are numerous in the distant Yorkshire Wolds, where there is plenty of flint to create local tools. Over a dozen have even turned up in the River Thames, suggesting the Langdale axe was not only an early success of British engineering, but a must-have Neolithic object.[2]

When writing of Castlerigg, Ann Radcliffe imagined the stone circle, in true Gothic fashion, as a place of "midnight festival" and "savage sacrifice". Centuries later, we picture the monument as a spectacular trading post, where tools shaped in high and remote quarries were once exchanged, receiving a potent ritual charge of stone-circle energy in the process. If folk from the southern flatlands did assemble here on a summer's afternoon to pick out some precious new items, we can only wonder at what they made of such a grand setting. A long journey indeed, but to arrive at such an impressive venue to obtain your charmed object would have been a worthy quest.

WALKING NOTES

You can park on the road that passes the circle (NY 29145 23634) but this does get busy, especially at weekends. For an extended ramble, it is possible to walk from nearby Keswick, using part of the old railway line path (watch out for the busy roads when plotting this route). The nearby Keswick Climbing Wall has a good café for an emergency cuppa if required.

BRYN CELLI DDU

Ritual continuity on the island of the Druids

ISLE OF ANGLESEY, WALES (SH 50753 70181)
OS EXPLORER 263

One evening thousands of years ago, within a sacred henge on the island now known in Welsh as Ynys Môn and in English as Anglesey, a ceremony was held. A pit had been dug at the centre of the henge, inside which a fire burned brightly, illuminating the celebrants and casting shifting shadows that reached out to the standing stones encircling the ritual. Before the fire was lit, a small bone from a human ear had been placed at its base. The ear bone heard the songs sung beneath the moon, the words said for the ancestors. When the flames died, the smouldering remains were covered with earth and a slab was set down beside the pit. This stone was especially important – patterned with sensuous, serpentine swirls, it had previously stood tall on the site, but was now committed to the ground. The pit cooled and the stone slept. Both would be unearthed five thousand years later, during the excavation of Bryn Celli Ddu in the 1920s.

The pit ceremony and the toppling of the Pattern Stone was the latest development in this site's history as a place of deep spiritual significance for Anglesey's prehistoric people. Five timber posts were erected here during the Mesolithic period, long before the henge was built, echoing those raised before the building of Stonehenge, and further changes were to come, as soon the stone circle would be felled, with some uprights being deliberately broken into fragments. In place of the stones, a wondrous passage grave was raised, a structure that would have dwarfed the reconstructed mound that now remains. Bryn Celli Ddu is a story of shifting ritual practice, of reimagining sacred space, but always in this place – the people who raised, adapted and destroyed monuments on the site agreed on one thing: this was a powerful spot.

Today, the passage grave feels pleasingly hidden, accessed by a footpath that tracks the rippling Afon Braint before turning through a labyrinth of tall hedgerows, hinting at the monument's name: "the mound in the dark grove". The landscape soon emerges once more as rolling hills and cow fields, interspersed here and there with deciduous woodland. A dairy farm sits alongside the site, adding to the sense of prosaic coexistence with the ancient that is evident all over Anglesey. This reaches surreal levels at Tŷ Mawr Standing Stone and the chambered tomb of Trefignath on Holy Island, which boast views of a lorry park, a former aluminium works and a massive Morrisons.

Although Bryn Celli Ddu would have been larger in its prime, it is still an incredibly impressive and beautifully proportioned structure, with the current grassy mound rising from its surrounding ditch to cover the monument's passageway and burial chamber. The entrance is flanked by sizeable megaliths, so that access to the passageway is gained by weaving between uprights. The experience inside the passage is uncanny – the quality of light within and the tone of the surrounding rock is dependent on the time of day, and indeed year, that you visit. Most potent of all is the midsummer solstice, with which the monument is aligned. On this auspicious morning, a beam of light from the rising sun enters the passage and illuminates the face of a particularly quartz-rich stone within the burial chamber. When it was freshly cut, this stone would have bounced light across the cavity. It is no exaggeration to say that to witness the solstice here is to see light fall as the ancients intended.

Although human remains have been recovered from the burial chamber and the passage, the mound's status as a burial site is difficult to determine, as early antiquarian investigations mean many bones may have been lost. Nevertheless, this was certainly a sacred resting place, a place where the dead could be warmed by the midsummer sun. The departed

were also provided with what archaeologist Aubrey Burl referred to as a "protectress", in the form of a roughly circular pillar in the chamber that can have the heart-stopping effect of appearing human-like to those who do not anticipate its presence. In the early nineteenth century the Reverend John Skinner told the tale of a farmer who was looting the site for stone "when lo! in a chamber at the further end a figure in white seemed to forbid his approach. The poor man had scarcely power sufficient to crawl backwards out of this den of spirits."[1] In more recent years, the archaeologist Steve Burrow has also written of this companion of the dead, noting that the pillar was erected in a spot which is never illuminated. When the sun's light hits the chamber's rear wall, the silent guardian watches from the shadows.[2]

Elsewhere in Burrow's article, he argues persuasively that there could never have been a stone circle or henge on the site. It was, rather, a passage tomb from the start. Furthermore, the Pattern Stone was not stood upright to be admired, but always buried as the "symbolic heart" of this

The nearby Bryn-yr-Hen-Bobl chambered cairn

building project, which was intended to capture the rays of the solstice – a process carried out for the dead and overseen by their protectress. Perhaps that burning ritual was to dedicate the tomb's initial construction rather than to mark the passing of the stone circle. Regardless of the phases of the monument's construction, however, there must have been a deep connection to this location, influencing and inspiring the monument's builders and visitors over a significant time period.

The full scale of the ritual context surrounding Bryn Celli Ddu is still emerging. In addition to the nearby Tyddyn-bach Standing Stone, an unusual outcrop visible from the mound has yielded prehistoric rock art, while evidence of a huge burial mound to the south of the site has recently been unearthed. When watching the summer sun rise over and within the tomb, there is a sense that there is much more to be discovered within this rich landscape of the ancestors. The ear bone, now charred and aged, is listening again.

"Bryn Celli Ddu is a story of shifting ritual practice, of reimagining sacred space, but always in this place"

WALKING NOTES

There is a small car park for Bryn Celli Ddu (SH 50500 69870). The site is signposted from the car park and is only around 0.5km (550 yards) away along a gravel path. There are plenty of options to map a longer walk to tie in with a visit to Bryn Celli Ddu. Footpaths for the Wales Coastal Path and Isle of Anglesey Coastal Path run nearby. The beautiful Bodowyr dolmen (SH 46223 68170) is 6km (3.7 miles) away. With Snowdon in the distance behind the monument, it's just one of many impressive sites on Anglesey.

AVEBURY

Time collapses within the world's largest stone circle

WILTSHIRE, ENGLAND [SU 10201 69962]
OS EXPLORER 157

Avebury is a gathering place. For millennia since the sarsen stones were dragged here and stood on end to form its great temple, and likely for millennia before that, people have been drawn to this spot. Within the epic Neolithic wonderland that spills out from the remnants of the World Heritage Site's stone circles, are long barrows, mounds, avenues and sacred springs of global renown. As the archaeologist Francis Pryor writes of Avebury's landscape, "It's hard to know where to start."[1] And people, of course, still arrive at Avebury. Now a perfect English settlement uniquely located within a henge, it is both a neatly maintained tourist destination and a highly charged centre of re-enchantment.

Unlike its Wiltshire neighbour, the Neolithic winter temple of Stonehenge, Avebury is a place of summer. In June especially this parish pulses with life. It is there in the wildflower meadows and overgrown hedgerows where greenery bursts forth, following spring's annual soaking. However, beneath this layer of rural charm lies a deep well of memory, an underbelly of psychic power accreted over centuries of ritual life that rises to the surface on the longest day. Lying on the grass among the stones following a pint at the Red Lion (the only pub in the known world to be located inside a stone circle), the vibe is hard to

121

top. The ancients knew what they were doing, building here. Their structures maximised the unity between the individual and the landscape, a unity that reaches its peak on the summer solstice.

At this potent time, many disparate groups of travellers (New Age and old), Druids, pagans, ravers, ramblers, witches, wizards, morris dancers, musicians and folk of all kinds descend upon the stone circles to welcome the sunrise. The joyful polyphony of chants and drums, the faraway bass of the sound systems on the ancient Ridgeway path and the excited buzz of the crowd soused in cider and psilocybin build steadily following the setting of the sun, gaining momentum through the night until finally offering up a celebratory release as the sun rises above the henge. This is only the current incarnation of an age-old observance, one which serves to connect us to the seasons and those who have gone before.

Avebury's bold midsummer magic is particularly evident when standing between two remarkable stones near the centre of the

> "Our ancestors congregated here, and people continue to do so thousands of years later, among the vibes and the verifiable, the ancient and the modern"

northern circle, known as the cove. These point to Hackpen Hill and that key solstice sunrise, and it's easy to imagine this spot as the most sacred space of all. If you look closely at one of the cove stones, you can see a face in the rock. This startling feature is either a masterpiece of Neolithic art or another ancient case of pareidolia.

Either way, it certainly speaks to an idea that may well lie at the heart of Avebury's appeal: that of humans and megaliths intertwined. Avebury is not the only site to juxtapose ancient stones with more recent additions, but this village has coexisted with its monuments from time immemorial: a venerable community amid a Neolithic temple. At the time of Domesday Book, the circles had already been standing for close to 4,000 years. Throughout their existence, the stones have been both sanctified and scorned by the local populace, the monuments shifting as many were destroyed and buried, only to be resurrected when much

of Avebury was recreated by Scottish businessman and archaeologist Alexander Keiller in the 1930s.

Alongside juxtaposition, another key thread that runs through Avebury's monuments is transformation. Derek Jarman's flickering, saturated 1971 film, *A Journey to Avebury*, conjures the Wiltshire countryside as a twilit dreamscape where Avebury's stones loom like ageless sentinels, as though Arthur C. Clarke's Monoliths have been dropped into an English summer idyll of deep yellows and greens. There is an indefinable something about the stones that suggests powerful agency, as if, much like those artefacts from *Space Odyssey*, they have the ability to trigger some kind of change in those who encounter them. For visitors to Avebury, the laying of hands upon stones is intuitive (and more or less mandatory).

This transformative theme can be seen in depictions of Avebury throughout the seventies. In Mary Rayner's 1975 children's novel, *The Witchfinder*, the village is restyled as Wansbury, and the megaliths are responsible for turning the main character's mother into a witch. Two years later, Avebury was famously used to stage the TV serial *Children of the Stones*, this time fictionalised as Milbury, wherein astrophysicist Adam Brake and his psychically gifted son Matthew must outwit sinister forces and learn the secret of the stones, channelling the circle's mysterious power to free the village from a perpetual time loop. And in a more adult tale of witchy possession, the same year's *Stigma* formed part of the BBC's *Ghost Story for Christmas* strand, the moving of a megalith releasing an uncontrollable malevolent energy.

The stones certainly resonated with the culture of that haunted decade, and they continue to exert a pull on artists, writers and mystical adventurers today. Whereas in fiction this draw is often a darkly powerful one, in reality many find the site fills them with a positive charge, and several influential figures, from the artist Paul Nash to Archdrude Julian Cope, have immersed themselves in the complex. Even trailblazing pop mastermind Joe Meek (of "Telstar" fame) encountered the stones while spending his National Service working on radar at RAF Yatesbury. It was here, only a few miles from Avebury's circles, Meek honed his electronics skills, and perhaps hints

Archdrude
Julian Cope

125

of his time in megalithic Wiltshire can be heard in the rocking stomp of his 1962 act, the Stonehenge Men.

Standing here in the present moment, among nineteenth-century farm buildings adapted for National Trust use, and 30-tonne megaliths erected 5,000 years before that – within sight of manicured Edwardian topiary and the apple trees of Avebury Manor garden – is to acknowledge that any kind of linear history is insufficient for Avebury. You simply need to savour the enchantment such high levels of atemporal disorder encourages. There is, however, one constant shining through the ages like the rising solstice sun. Our ancestors congregated here, and people continue to do so thousands of years later, among the vibes and the verifiable, the ancient and the modern. It is no accident that the great concentration of monuments in and around the Avebury complex still functions as a place of pilgrimage. The ancients devised it as such.

WALKING NOTES

There is a large car park at SU 09964 69603. This gets very busy at summer solstice and it may be worth walking in from further out or using public transport. Avebury's massive outer circle is nearly impossible to comprehend at ground level. We would recommend taking the time to trace the perimeter of the henge, following the stones clockwise from the main National Trust complex (SU 10014 70021), in order to mentally calibrate the scale. Some access is restricted periodically due to erosion, but in summer months a full circumambulation can more or less be achieved, interrupted only by the busy Swindon Road.

The aforementioned National Trust area features exhibitions in the barn alongside the usual café, toilets and shop. The Alexander Keiller museum is well worth a look, as is Avebury Manor (SU 09904 69997), which was used in the filming of *Children of the Stones*. The Red Lion pub can be found at SU 10201 69962. Among the lore associated with this ancient hostelry is one particularly gruesome tale, which tells of a seventeenth-century woman named Florrie who was strangled and thrown down the village well. The covered well is now inside the pub, where it doubles as a grisly drinks table; Florrie's spirit is said to haunt the building, looking for her murderous husband.

Walking out from Avebury village allows you to access Silbury Hill (approx. 2km/1.2 miles away) and the wider ritual landscape. Also within walking distance are the wonderful Adam and Eve stones near Avebury Trusloe (SU 08907 69318), which formed part of a now-vanished avenue and cove.

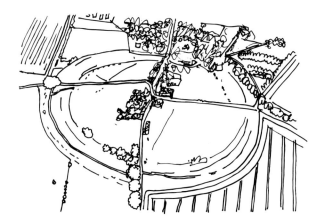

MIDMAR STONE CIRCLE

The pious and the pagan juxtaposed in the land of the recumbent stone circle

ABERDEENSHIRE, SCOTLAND (NJ 69935 06489)
OS EXPLORER 406

Aberdeenshire is rightly famed for its recumbent stone circles. Unique to northeast Scotland, these remarkable arrangements feature a horizontal slab (the recumbent) flanked by two tall uprights within a circle of standing stones. The focal point of these monuments allows the imagination to run wild, giving the suggestive impression of a sacrificial altar, a deconstructed dolmen, or even inverted vampiric fangs. Visiting recumbent circles can become addictive, their deep and abiding mysteries often enhanced by beautiful natural settings, of which their builders were surely aware. The area around the town of Inverurie is particularly rich in recumbents, and one of the most resonant and vibe-filled is located, strangely, in Midmar Kirk – a peculiar palimpsest where the hoary vestiges of a profane past have been reframed by the incoming new religion, rather than rewritten.

Approaching the remote church on a summer morning and climbing a hill spattered with yellow gorse, unusually bright rays scatter through the trees that line the site's perimeter. Everything here is trimmed and neat – sky-blue gates match the church window frames and door, while carefully planted daffodil patches brighten the lawn. Rounding the building, however, turns the scene on its head:

here stands one of Aberdeenshire's most enchanting stone circles, right next to the church. The juxtaposition of this outlandish pagan monument with the modest order of the kirk is striking, and worth some heavy rumination while relaxing in the circle's grassy middle. Despite losing some stones and suffering reconstructive tinkering over the years, these megaliths retain a strange power, and there is something eerily animalistic about the massive recumbent and its flankers. Julian Cope saw them as a "gigantic horned-god rising out of the living earth" – and once you have that in your head, it's hard to shake the impression that an ancient, sleeping beast of stone lurks below the graveyard, ready to rise up Ray Harryhausen-style and consume the church next door.[1] Such demonic thoughts were already on the mind of one nineteenth-century commentator who described the flankers in dramatic, biblical terms as "the horns of the altar".[2]

131

"Visiting recumbent circles can become addictive, their deep and abiding mysteries often enhanced by beautiful natural settings, of which their builders were surely aware"

However, the circle's churchyard setting is not one that fits the old narrative of religious dominance, where it was supposed that many medieval British churches were built upon places of ancient pagan sanctity. This theory has been increasingly questioned by historians and archaeologists, who have found very few cases where monuments were directly co-opted or built over.[3] If the medieval view of ancient sites can seem one of indifference, a great deal more interest was summoned in the eighteenth century, when the new Midmar Kirk was built. This was a time of antiquarian speculation about the purposes of megalithic monuments, and the explosion of modern Druidry. Perhaps surprisingly, by no means all Christian authorities were opposed to Druidic thinking and engagement with prehistoric sites in this period – in fact, Midmar Kirk may well have been deliberately positioned to benefit from its association with the circle, rather than overshadow it. Vibes absorbed, not erased.

John Ogilvie, Midmar's minister at the time of the church's relocation closer to the stones in 1787, was a poet who loved the recumbent circles of the area, writing floridly in praise of the monuments – "Ordained with earth's revolving orb to last! Thou bringst to sight the present and the past."[4] Ogilvie was no doubt aware of the work of the great English antiquarian William Stukeley, who did so much early work on Stonehenge and Avebury, and whose illustrations of megaliths in the landscape remain important and wondrous documents. Stukeley wasn't averse to grand, mystical readings of the monuments he studied, and directly linked Druidic religion to Christianity, writing, "The Druids were of Abraham's religion intirely, at least in the earliest times, and worshipp'd the supreme Being in the same manner as he did."[5] This kind of thinking allowed churchmen interested in numinous pagan ruins the opportunity to have their megalithic cake and eat it, and perhaps Ogilvie saw in the building of a new church the opportunity to make a physical connection to ancient British religion as he and Stukeley interpreted it. Ogilvie understood the power of enchantment, and wanted to co-opt it for his church.

Stukeley's biblical interpretations don't hold much sway today, but the original purpose of Scotland's recumbent stone circles is still very much debated. One theory that does ring true links the sites to the lunar calendar, fascinatingly interpreting the circles as places of the moon rather than the sun. In this view, the altar and its horns formed a kind of widescreen TV within which auspicious lunar events could be framed. As the recumbent circles date primarily from the Bronze Age, perhaps they show an evolution from solar-powered Neolithic practices to later moonlit rituals. The idea is supported not only by lunar alignments, but by what are known as cupmarks on some recumbents, which could well represent astronomical observations. These markings can clearly be seen on the large stone of a nearby circle, the wonderfully named Sunhoney, which is tucked away behind farm buildings about a mile from Midmar. Sunhoney is well worth a visit, and sits in stark contrast to Midmar's manicured setting. Here, surrounded by a ring of trees, the long grass and ancient tree stumps lend the monument an undiscovered feel. It's a beautiful, peaceful spot for contemplation, with the trees in full leaf and the climbing sun coaxing ever shorter shadows from the stones. The farm sets a great example too, welcoming visitors and keeping the circle accessible.

There are other gems hidden in this landscape. Just across the car park north of Midmar Kirk, lies a small, Tolkienesque wood, dominated by a venerable, spreading beech. Following the winding path through the trees reveals a tall and slender standing stone, which is said to resemble a rearing serpent or an engorged phallus (take your pick). Perhaps this loner was an outlier connected to the Midmar circle; its presence certainly complements an already mythic landscape. The eighteenth-century church fits in here too, part of a palimpsest that also features the ruins of Midmar Old Kirk and an Iron Age hillfort on nearby Barmekin Hill. As a summer night draws close, the stone circle next to Midmar's church anticipates the moonlight to come. And on this cool evening it is possible to reconcile two very different structures, and perhaps agree with the artist Marianna Lines's view that "the potent atmosphere created by the marriage of the two enriches the present".[6]

WALKING NOTES
Midmar Kirk and its circle can be found at NJ 69935 06489. There is a small car park behind the church. 2.5km (1.6 miles) away, Sunhoney Farm can be accessed by a track at NJ 71743 05387. Walk past the farm buildings and turn left at NJ 71768 05636, following the length of the stone wall to the Sunhoney stone circle at NJ 71595 05702.

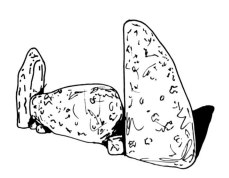

THE HURLERS

A spectral network of stone circles and ley line energies

```
CORNWALL (SX 25813 71390)
OS EXPLORER 109
```

Cornwall is a narrative landscape and nowhere, perhaps, is this truer than up on Bodmin. Within these eighty square miles of granite moorland are a remarkable collection of natural features and ancient sites that frame a vibrant canvas of folklore, myth and mystery.

Setting off early to the moor village of Minions from nearby Liskeard, the direction of travel is notably uphill. The summer can swelter on the moor and an early start beats the sun and any crowds. The village is quiet at this time, although plenty of sheep still rampage around the main thoroughfare, while ponies and their foals lounge in the shade.

After leaving the car park, the magnificent triple ring of the Hurlers soon comes into view. The stones have been known by their current name since the sixteenth century at least, an accompanying tale telling of the sport of hurling being played on the Sabbath and the offending participants being, somewhat predictably, turned to stone. Such stories were born towards the end of the Middle Ages and re-energised by Puritans following the Reformation. That this hoary tale may be a little glitchy is indicated by the Pipers, two beautiful standing stones found not far from the Hurlers. Perhaps the Pipers once provided the music for a petrified dance, as at Stanton Drew (see page 93), before the story shifted to include the traditional Cornish sport of hurling. Either way, here the stones and their connections are far more interesting than their etymology.

The Hurlers was undoubtedly a special place. The twenty-eight stones within the largest, central circle (fourteen remain) were given the royal treatment, smoothed by hammering and carefully aligned with the nearby Rillaton Barrow. The northern circle retains fifteen stones, and there is evidence of a quartz causeway linking this group to the central configuration. A recently discovered fallen stone has been suggested as the start point of a processional route across the site, reinforcing its sacred significance.[1] It is a remarkable thing to walk between three ancient stone circles within such a small area. Even though the ruined

"It is a remarkable thing to walk between three ancient stone circles within such a small area"

southern circle has only two stones standing, you still get a definite sense of magic within this triple hit of a site.

Alignments buzz around here too. The aforementioned connection to Rillaton Barrow isn't the only link in the chain. The engineer and researcher Alexander Thom would propose not only solar alignments within the Hurlers, but also that some stones had been positioned to consider the stars Vega and Arcturus.[2] A more extravagant claim was made by the countercultural thinker John Michell, who had a great love of Cornish sites. For Michell, the Hurlers were part of the St Michael Line, a mythic corridor running through southwest England. An alignment of sites far longer than any regular ley line, this was a dragon path – a potent energy channel, rich in poetic allegory. Many of the aligned locations are linked to dragon slaying saints, a connection Michell inferred as a relic memory of the line's original purpose: carrying the mysterious, life-giving dragon force (see also Silbury Hill, page 258).

There is something in the air, in the ground, at the Hurlers – a certain charge. Walking to the Pipers, another landscape connection emerges. The uprights clearly outline the imposing bulk of Stowe's Hill, its unusual rock formations just visible alongside the scars of quarrying. For a people so connected to the land, such framing can surely not have been coincidental.

The stroll from the Pipers towards Stowe's Hill is a pleasant one, passing buildings from Cornwall's mining past and, as you fork towards the outcrop, hawthorn trees are to be found scattered among the ferns. Climbing the hill, you are immediately aware of the enormous, bizarre granite character of the Cheesewring. Sculpted by untold millennia of weathering, the formation was aptly described by Wilkie Collins: "If a man dreamt of a great pile of stones in a nightmare, he would dream of such a pile as the Cheesewring."[3] It seems the stories begin to improve the further out on the moor you wander: no simple petrified remains explain the Cheesewring's origins.

The tale runs that when Christianity was first introduced to Cornwall, the saints consecrated the wells and raised up stone crosses on the moor. Such intrusion into the landscape annoyed the local giants to the point that one of them, Uther, was tasked with ridding Cornwall of the newcomers. When the diminutive St Tue caught wind of this, he challenged Uther to a stone-hurling competition. The giant laughed – he knew his luck was in. If Tue lost, he and his number would leave the moor, and if Uther lost, every giant would convert to Christianity. The contest began, and soon a strange pile of enormous stones was piling up on Stowe's Hill, the agreed target. With some divine intervention (cheating, surely?), Tue held his own so that it all came down to the last throw. Uther's final rock smashed against the side of the hill and the giant wailed in dismay. It was left to Tue to toss the final, heaviest stone onto the towering pile, and he was helped once again in his actions, this time by an angel. Uther was so impressed he offered himself up for

John "ley lines" Michell

"Sculpted by untold millennia of weathering, the formation was aptly described by Wilkie Collins: "If a man dreamt of a great pile of stones in a nightmare, he would dream of such a pile as the Cheesewring.""

baptism immediately. Soon, his gigantic companions followed suit or left Cornwall in disgust at the saint's victory.[4]

Sitting beneath the Cheesewring and appreciating its welcome shade, it is easy to see how folklore would accumulate around such an incredible formation. This outcrop is one of several similar, erratic natural features on top of the hill. There is evidence of manmade structures up here too. Stowe's Pound consists of two enormous prehistoric stone walls, breathtaking in their scale. Another enclosure to the north has been found to contain over one hundred hut circles. While admiring the view, it's possible to imagine a very real connection between these ancient people and the monuments on the moor below.

From Stowe's Hill, the path can be re-joined briefly before heading across the open moor towards Rillaton Barrow, another place of stories. The largest round barrow on Bodmin Moor, Rillaton's distinctive capstone can be seen peeking through the turf along with its supporting uprights. Shining a torch into the darkness reveals a small, mysterious chamber. When the barrow was excavated in 1837, a remarkable item was among the finds. This was the Rillaton gold cup, an incredible piece of

craftsmanship, dated to 1700 BCE and now in the British Museum (after a spell on George V's dressing table, housing his collar studs). The cup's unearthing reflected a strange local tale. It was said that the ghost of a Druid priest would sit atop his stone seat on Stowe's Hill and offer drink to wanderers on the moor. Travellers would drink a delicious liquid from the Druid's cup and it would magically refill for his next thirsty visitor. However, a local hunter once became so enraged that he could not empty the vessel that he threw the contents at the Druid and made off with the gold cup on his horse. Not a good move, as his horse soon faltered, throwing the hunter headfirst into a ravine, where he died. The story tells that the Rillaton gold cup was buried next to the man, whose bones were eventually found in the barrow alongside the Druid's chalice. There is no record of the tale before the excavation, of course, but we like to think that folk on the moor have long memories.

WALKING NOTES
There is a car park for the Hurlers on the edge of Minions (SX 25990 71100). The village itself has a café, a shop and public toilets as well as another car park. The pub, the Cheesewring Hotel, was being renovated following a fire when we visited.

To follow the route described above, it's a brief walk from the Hurlers car park to the stone circles (SX 25813 71390). The Pipers stand alongside at SX 25709 71355. From here, you can use the track to walk to a junction at SX 25427 71880, taking a right towards Stowe's Hill. At SX 25749 72226, you can take a path to a route up to the Cheesewring. We began the climb at SX 25692 72339 (take care on the rocks and avoid the quarry area, fenced off for safety). Once back down, you can walk across the open moor towards Rillaton Barrow (SX 26027 71909). From the barrow, head back to the Hurlers across the moor.

There are several other powerful sites in the area. The spectacular dolmen of Trethevy Quoit (pictured opposite) can be found at SX 25934 68811, with limited parking at SX 25980 68830 (4.5km/2.8 miles from the Hurlers). King Doniert's Stone (SX 23612 68847) is 3.7km (2.3 miles) from the Hurlers. It was erected in memory of Dungarth, the last king of Cornwall, who drowned in 875.

WHITE HORSE HILL

An embarrassment of legends and prehistoric riches in a timeless landscape

OXFORDSHIRE, ENGLAND (SU 30142 86613)
OS EXPLORER 170

When XTC songwriter Andy Partridge explained why the Uffington White Horse was emblazoned on the front of the group's new album, *English Settlement*, in 1982, he referred to a homecoming. The band had been on tour for years and, for a group of Swindon natives, this weirdly beautiful image represented a reconnection with their roots. In these parts, the Horse is embedded within local identity, its sinuous lines appearing on everything from school uniforms to pint glasses. The spirit of the place gallops up on White Horse Hill, and so Partridge's choice for his group's most English and pastoral collection to date made a lot of sense.

The White Horse's design is unique among hill figures. A strange, beaked head leads an abstract body composed of minimal strokes, somehow conveying a sense of movement. On a summer's day, its bright chalk form seems all too ready to sprint off, as in one theory of its purpose, to pull the sun across the sky. However, the most remarkable aspect of the Horse is that it is a living monument. For it to still be seen, and cherished on screen savers and album covers, it needs to be scoured, removing the grasses and weeds that encroach upon it. The White Horse gives this community its identity, but without the community it will disappear. With excavations in the 1990s dating the figure to the period between the fourteenth and sixth centuries

145

BCE, we can say that this reciprocal relationship has been enacted for thousands of years.[1]

And enacted joyously – the scouring was once a raucous carnival, involving cheese rolling, stick fighting and pig chasing competitions, alongside plenty of ale. Although it is now sedately managed by the National Trust, this annual summer event retains some of its old magic.

It is, after all, a proven survival of an ancient pagan custom happening right under our noses. A vital link to the ancestors.

The view from the Horse has changed a fair amount since the Bronze Age, but it remains an enchanting one. The strange folds of the valley known as the Manger, caused by retreating ice at the end of the last glacial period, give the landscape a fantastical appearance. Folklore holds that the White Horse gallops down to this Manger at night to satisfy its enormous appetite. And, if you happen to be upon White Horse Hill after sunset, with the figure gleaming in the moonlight, you can certainly believe such a thing possible.

"Like many of our ancient monuments, to stand at Wayland's Smithy is to be confronted with context, to orient yourself within what is — for us as human beings — deep time"

Next to the Manger's unusual rippled form is Dragon Hill – another mysterious spoke in this area's mythological wheel. The chalk mound is a natural feature, but its top seems to have been artificially levelled. The mound's name is drawn from local lore that identifies the summit as the place where St George slew his dragon. Here, you can touch the patch of bare chalk that signifies the beast's demise – for where dragon's blood is spilled no living thing can grow.

On walking back up to the brow of White Horse Hill, the imposing hillfort of Uffington Castle is soon revealed, its double banks providing substantial protection and, more recently, extreme sledging opportunities for local youngsters. As a peculiarly British indicator of Uffington Castle's size, you could fit six football pitches inside its earthen walls, although

147

Uffington United wisely choose to play their home games down the hill at Fawler Road.[2]

Some would suggest that the hillfort and the Horse, which is a mere spit away, are inextricably linked. Excavation has shown that Uffington Castle was constructed at the beginning of the Iron Age in the eighth century BCE. Although it commands fine views over the surrounding area and the hillfort undoubtedly has defensive features, archaeologists debate its purpose: rather than a military location, perhaps this was a ritual centre, a place to feast and connect with the old gods.

The abode of one of these gods can be found nearby. From White Horse Hill, a short, dusty stroll along the ancient Ridgeway track provides a worthy detour to a jewel of this landscape: the wondrous Neolithic tomb that has been known since Anglo-Saxon times as Wayland's Smithy. Rightly one of the most well-known long barrows in the country, its location is part of its appeal – with its great mass hunkered low in a picturesque grove of beeches it's the perfect spot for a magical recharge.

The barrow's name refers to the master blacksmith of Germanic myth, called Wēland in Old English and Völund in Old Norse. The story that accompanies his Smithy is long established in local lore: it is said that if a traveller's horse has lost its shoe, they can bring their steed to the barrow and leave it overnight with a silver coin as payment. At daybreak the coin will be gone, but the horse will have the finest shoe in England, crafted by the legendary smith himself.

Many have told the tale, but perhaps the weirdest interpretation can be found in the stripped-down psychedelia of Julian Cope's song "Wayland's Smithy Has Wings". In Cope's take on the legend, Wayland descends with his forge in a celestial juggernaut to shoe the horse of a flashy knight. Wayland is not easily impressed, however; and upon inspecting the amount offered in return for his services, he shoots back into the sky in disdain.

You may need to put down some serious cash to get a good horseshoe from Wayland these days, but you can take in his Smithy for free, and what a place it is: a chalk and earth mound of some 55m (180ft) surrounded by a belt of sarsen stones, with the burial chamber itself flanked by four huge sarsens. The first monument on the site was built at some point between

Hand tools used for the annual scouring of the White Horse, (opposite page) Druids form a sacred circle at Uffington

3590 and 3555 BCE and would have been an uncanny sight. It is thought that sarsen stones were laid below a large wooden box in which human remains were interred, while tree trunks were split and used to bookend the monument. By 3400 BCE a large barrow had been built over this first tomb and the imposing megaliths of its façade had been added. For around one hundred years people were buried in this second structure, which may well have been inspired by the famous long barrow at nearby West Kennet. And then the silence of millennia. Like many of our ancient monuments, to stand at Wayland's Smithy is to be confronted with

"This land, its monuments and rituals speak to a sense of respect between humans and their landscape, an under-standing and trust in the old places and the natural world that harbours them"

context, to orient yourself within what is – for us as human beings – deep time.

Strolling back along the Ridgeway towards White Horse Hill in the afternoon sun allows for some reflection upon this golden land and its prehistoric path. Parts of the trail beneath your feet have been walked for at least 5,000 years, the chalk ridges offering ideal routes for travel and trade, avoiding forests and waterlogged land. The Ridgeway, in all of its current 139km (86 miles) of glory, is a path of reconnection; and even this small section feels like a walk with those who have gone before.

Paths, like white horses, and traditions, can be lost in the absence of care. This land, its monuments and rituals speak to a sense of respect

Standing stones flank the trapezoid barrow at Wayland's Smithy

between humans and their landscape, an understanding and
trust in the old places and the natural world that harbours them.
The pre-industrial people understood this, and their annual
customs reinforced it. Standing on this hill on a summer's evening
generates a nagging thought: if the White Horse vanishes, so
will we.

WALKING NOTES

The land around White Horse Hill is perfect for a ramble, and
you'll find numerous circular walks in the area. Parking for the
hill figure can be found at SU 29332 86564. From here you can
walk to the White Horse at SU 30142 86613, although you'll get a
better view from down at Dragon Hill (SU 30069 86860), which
also makes a fine picnic stop. You can get onto the Ridgeway
by first visiting Uffington Castle and its trig point at SU 30076
86384. Join at SU 30099 86259 and carry on towards Wayland's
Smithy at SU 28146 85323.

151

AUTUMN

As the wheel of the year turns, we enter a transformative, sensory season of wood smoke and leaf litter, warm gloves and fireworks.

We journey from genteel harvest festivals and apple-bobbing on village greens to conflagrations of flaming tar barrels carried aloft through darkening streets, and effigies razed to ashes on community bonfires. Slowly but surely, autumn shows us the unravelling of order, with mischief and mayhem surging within its venerable traditions.

The gathering of the harvest is still celebrated across these islands, and in Kent we see monuments such as Coldrum Long Barrow, built by Britain's earliest farmers and with crops still gathered in its lengthening shadow. Elsewhere, as the last of nature's abundance is stored away for the lean months ahead, old ways usher in dark days through strange, revenant forms – from the Abbots Bromley Horn Dance to the raucous fires of Ottery St Mary and Lewes, with their echoes of ancient Samhain rites. Like spring, this is a season when light and dark momentarily balance, but now when the scales tilt, it is towards the night.

It is often said that in autumn the veil between our world and what lies beyond is at its thinnest. We feel these liminal vibes at work at Oxfordshire's Rollright Stones, threaded as

155

they are with dark folklore, and out on Norfolk's windswept
limit, where E. F. Benson found a distinctly haunted landscape.
But this is also a moment of wondrous natural beauty, and now
the heat of summer has passed, one of our favourite times
to get outside for a wander. Certain sites are particularly
attuned to the season, such as the wooded stone circle of
Doll Tor, or the prehistoric landscape that lurks within the
plantation of Fernworthy Forest on Dartmoor. No matter where
you tread within this in-between season, however, the layers of
history and mystery will be close at hand.

SELECTED AUTUMN OBSERVANCES:
· Crying the Neck in Cornwall — September (at the end of
  the harvest)
· Braughing Old Man's Day — 2 October
· Ackworth Harvest Sheaf — Sunday in early October
· Boscastle All Hallows (the Dark Gathering) — Saturday on
  or before 31 October
· Edinburgh Samhuinn Fire Parade — 31 October
· Lewes Bonfire — 5 November
· Shebbear Turning the Devil's Stone — 5 November
· Trefin St Martin's Fair and Mock Mayor — weekend in November

COLDRUM LONG BARROW

A magnificent megalithic power-up on the Pilgrims' Way

KENT, ENGLAND (TQ 65430 60723)
OS EXPLORER 148

The Pilgrims' Way is one of Britain's most famous trails and runs from Winchester in Hampshire to Canterbury in Kent. Once used by medieval pilgrims on their way to the shrine of Thomas Becket, the archbishop murdered in 1170, much of the original route lies beneath modern roads. A sense of the journey can still be gained, however, by trekking along the North Downs Way, which tends to follow the Pilgrims' Way where it can or run on the higher ground above the roads. The approximate route is much older than Christianity itself, and its vicinity is scattered with the remnants of a more ancient culture. It also passes through some seriously evocative landscapes; as the historian of the Pilgrims' Way, Julia Cartwright, noted in 1911: "It is still a pleasant thing to ride out on a spring or summer morning and follow the Pilgrims' Way. For the scenes through which it leads are fair, and the memories that it wakes belong to the noblest pages of England's story."[1] Just off the Pilgrims' Way, in deepest Kent, lies the most magnificent of the Medway Megaliths, Coldrum Long Barrow.

On an autumn afternoon, a walk in these parts is the perfect power-up, connecting the rambler not only to a compelling ancient site, but also to a trackway and an agricultural tradition whose legacies endure. If strolling to Coldrum from its small car park, you follow a path that winds through

thickets of woodland and along field edges. Before harvest, these acres are packed with peas, a rolling sea of green, while blackberries grow fat in the hedgerows. The fingerposts eventually lead you to the barrow itself, which is revealed slowly as you climb the steps up to the ridge upon which the monument was constructed. When looking out at the colossal remains of the rectangular burial chamber, once misidentified as a stone circle, the view is wondrous. Fields roll to the horizon, and a wooded chalk escarpment climbs sharply to your left, the Pilgrims' Way hugging its base.

Sign from 1926 misidentifying the burial chamber as a stone circle

Coldrum is one of Britain's oldest megalithic structures, belonging to the earliest phase of the Neolithic in these isles, when farming and the construction of magnificent tomb shrines were at the cutting edge of the culture. People were buried here in two phases running over hundreds of years, beginning almost six thousand years ago. Although much of the barrow has been robbed during the course of its long history, it still has a unique power and complexity, its ruddy sarsen stones glowing beautifully in the fading sunlight.

Since the late twentieth century, modern pagans have also found this to be a sacred spot. Nearby tree branches are hung with rags and offerings, while one trunk is carved with runic inscriptions. When we visit, someone has drawn a pentagram in the ash of a small fire; an elderly couple are in deep contemplation on one of the kerb stones. Another, more unusual, feature appears to be an offering of crushed tortillas and After Eight Mints, but we aren't here to judge. The vibe is wonderfully calm, cleansing even.

What of the trackway that sits to the north of the long barrow? It may be that Mesolithic hunter-gatherers used the route of the Pilgrims' Way, along the chalk downland, thousands of years before Coldrum was built, as the glaciers retreated at the end of the last ice age.[2] The early Neolithic megalith builders would also have been familiar with the path, which perhaps once extended not to Winchester in the west, but to Salisbury Plain and the great ritual centre of Stonehenge. The location of the barrow could well be linked to the existence of the track. Indeed, it has been argued that some of the sites in the Medway were connected by processional routes, and that an avenue once led from Coldrum to the nearby dolmen of Kit's Coty, following the route of the Pilgrims' Way. In the twentieth century, ley line enthusiasts would find alignments of their own in the area, linking Coldrum to several local churches and suggesting that a legendary tunnel connecting Trottiscliffe church to the long barrow could well be a memory of this ley in action.[3] Whatever the truth of the Pilgrims' Way's role in the distant past, much like the Ridgeway that connects Wayland's Smithy and the Uffington White Horse (see page 145), walking this path is a direct line to the ancients.

In more recent times, the landscape around here has had more to do with beer than barrows. Kent is rightly renowned for its ale, and once hop gardens full of tall, climbing bines laden with bitter hop cones dotted the county. If Kent's Neolithic farmers were some of the first to bring agriculture and monument building to Britain, this innovative spirit was still around in the Tudor period, when Kent became the first county to harvest hops to flavour beer. The crop would be gathered during August and September by an army of

"Although much of the barrow has been robbed during the course of its long history, it still has a unique power and complexity, its ruddy sarsen stones glowing beautifully in the fading sunlight"

hop pickers, who often came from the capital. Around the primeval Medway Megaliths, Cockney voices would ring out in the fields, far from the pollution of the city. Life could still be tough out here, but many pickers would speak positively of the opportunity to head out to the countryside and earn some extra cash.[4]

Like many harvests, hop picking developed its own traditions, as the *Oxford Dictionary of English Folklore* explains:

> At the end of the picking season, the pickers chose a King and Queen from among their own number, who were dressed up in flowers and ribbons, and these two led the procession, which included hop-poles also decorated with ribbons, to a nearby barn, where they spent the evening merrymaking.[5]

These festivities were simply the latest incarnation of the harvest celebrations that have taken place across the world since the dawn of agriculture, thanking nature for its abundance. No doubt the early farmers who built Coldrum had their own rituals. In Canterbury, the final destination of the Pilgrims' Way, a traditional Hop Hoodening event takes place at the cathedral on the second Saturday in September each year. Local morris groups dance in the streets and the Hop Queen arrives, wearing a crown of cones and surrounded by decorative hop bines. Although mechanisation put an end to the mass migration of Londoners, the spirit of the hop harvest lives on in Kent. And, in September, a stroll in this landscape allows you to wind back the agricultural year not only to the hop pickers, but across thousands of years of toil, tradition and togetherness.

WALKING NOTES

There is a small car park down a tight lane at TQ 65005 60738. From here, follow the path to TQ 65373 60839, where a right turn will take you to the long barrow. To get onto the Pilgrims' Way, go back on yourself, up a magical hollow way, and then along the edge of a field to TQ 65259 61277. A good circular walk can be mapped that takes in Trosley Country Park, where there are further car parking options (TQ 63244 61066).

There is a decent chunk of folklore associated with Coldrum, not least the story of a "Black Prince" buried on the site, following his death in battle. A similar tale is told about Kit's Coty dolmen (TQ 74512 60846), another of the Medway Megaliths, some 14km (8.7 miles) to the east of Coldrum, which also sits just off the North Downs Way.

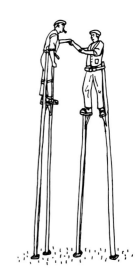

ABBOTS BROMLEY

A revenant stag ritual lives on in the heart of England

STAFFORDSHIRE, ENGLAND (SK 07914 24563)
OS EXPLORER 244

O n first acquaintance, the Staffordshire village of Abbots Bromley has a similar character to many affluent semi-rural settlements, where listed buildings rub shoulders with modern detached houses, and some folk indulge their *Grand Designs* pretensions. Work vans and elderly shoppers bustle in the centre; an ancient half-timbered pub does brisk lunchtime business in the autumn sunshine, while another, converted to an upmarket Indian restaurant, gears up for the evening rush.

This village, however, is the locus of a major temporal disruption, a revenant of the highest order. Each year, locals perform the Abbots Bromley Horn Dance, a deeply enigmatic tradition. The custom takes place on the Monday following the first Sunday after 4 September, and is utterly unique. Throughout the day of the ritual, six dancers carry pairs of reindeer antlers through the streets, and the group is joined by a Fool, a Maid Marian, a hobby horse, a bowman, a triangle player and an accordionist. The juxtaposition that this performance creates with quotidian twenty-first-century life is hard to overstate. Time buckles as the rite is enacted. The repetitive motion of the dancers' steps, and the repetition of these steps on this day through the centuries, create a pleasing loop. This is a timeline Abbots Bromley returns to annually.

165

Setting off from the parish church in the early morning, the team visits pubs, farms and other notable spots, dancing at each. During the dance, the horns are carried at chest height and tilted when two lines of dancers meet. As Steve Roud notes in *The English Year*, the Horn Dance is distinctly unpretentious and lacking in elaborate footwork. A 1936 report of the custom in *The Times* stated, "The whole thing is done unassumably and with a quiet purposefulness which is the keynote of the whole proceedings. One feels they are not dancing for joy or self-expression, but going quietly about a task which must be accomplished without unnecessary fuss."[1]

There is a sense of the marking of time, of a tradition that must be performed because it always has been, even though its origins are lost. The event today feels more upbeat and festive than 1930s witnesses attest, but the unhurried nature of the performance remains and is perhaps what makes the Horn Dance so haunting, especially in its final moments once the sun has set. The ritual's enchanting strangeness has made it a key folk horror reference – a custom embedded within a rural community that is beyond the comprehension of outsiders. In the 1970s, the eldritch power of the dance was seized upon by authors, and, as was the case in this haunted decade, it was often children, or at least young adults, who were the target audience for the ensuing weirdness.

Penelope Lively's *The Wild Hunt of Hagworthy* and Josephine Poole's *Billy Buck* sit alongside *Stag Boy* by William Rayner as children's novels that draw on aspects of the Horn Dance for inspiration. Rayner's lead character is even able to shapeshift into stag form, realising the potential of "playing the stag" – a mysterious practice that was railed against by medieval Christian authors in several parts of Europe. In the sixth century, the Bishop of Arles warned that these stag men "are not just playing a game but are instead raving in a sacrilegious rite".[2] Another churchman, writing in the ninth century, laid down the punishment for such wickedness: "If anyone on the kalends of January goes around as a stag or a heifer, that is, if they change themselves into the form of wild beasts and dress themselves in the skins of animals and don the heads of beasts ... three years penance, because it is devilish."[3] The lingering pagan overtones of ritual animal disguise were clearly unwelcome for many in the early medieval church; once again, man is conditioned to feel separate from nature.

The horns at Abbots Bromley have been carbon-dated to the time of the Norman Conquest. This adds to the intrigue,

as reindeer were most likely extinct in Britain by this time. Festivities in the Abbots Bromley area have been documented since 1226, and although the first specific reference to the Horn Dance comes in the seventeenth century, it may be much older. But what can we discern of the origin and meaning of the dance? As Ronald Hutton points out in *The Stations of the Sun*, it is difficult to make the case for the Horn Dance being an unreconstructed pagan survival, because it is such a strange and wonderful anomaly. In its combination of elements, it recalls no other known custom or tradition: "It is, in effect, an Abbots Bromley original, and all the more worthy of respect for that."[4]

One plausible explanation for the tradition lies in festive fundraising customs, such as hobby horse dances, which were

"The juxtaposition that this performance creates with quotidian twenty-first-century life is hard to overstate. Time buckles as the rite is enacted"

well established during midwinter by the Tudor period. Early mentions of the Abbots Bromley dance state that the event originally took place not in September but at Christmas, with the change of date linked to a period of inactivity before a revival in the eighteenth century. Winter customs frequently involve animal disguise, and antlers would have been an impressive addition. This view is bolstered by the fact that the earliest source to specifically mention "reindeer's heads" also refers to the collection of money for the poor and the upkeep of the church during the performance.

Perhaps the arrival of the horns in the village also stirred a folk memory of the shadowy ancient practice of playing the stag. The venerable hunting chase of Needwood Forest was on the village's doorstep, and wild animals would have loomed large in the mind of the medieval population in these parts. There is certainly an urge to "become the beast", a universal compulsion to disguise by echoing the animal kingdom, which has been felt since the dawn of time. We see it in the Mesolithic deer masks found at Star Carr in North Yorkshire, and, in more recent times, in the form of straw bears and hobby horses. However the horns arrived in Abbots Bromley, their magnetic draw turned out to be the perfect complement to the village's revelry. Their unique nature has probably ensured the survival of this remarkable

The accordion players of the Abbots Bromley dancers

tradition into the present, and may, we hope, inspire a revival of ritual animal disguise into the future.

WALKING NOTES
The day usually begins at St Nicholas' Church (SK 07914 24563) with the collection of the horns (which are housed in its north chapel) at 7.45am, followed by dancing on the village green. The dancers then move on to Yeatsall, followed by Admaston on the other side of the Blithfield Reservoir. A visit is paid to Blithfield Hall before heading back in the direction of Abbots Bromley and Little Dunstall Farm. A succession of pubs are visited in the village before the eerie finale in the evening and the return of the horns to the church at 8.15pm. There is parking in the village if you arrive early.

THE ROLLRIGHT STONES

A persistent vibe of witchy folklore clings to ancient stones

OXFORDSHIRE, ENGLAND (SP 29578 30873)
OS EXPLORER 191

Few sites exert an autumnal pull like the Rollright Stones, on the border between Oxfordshire and Warwickshire. The complex is entwined with fairies, witches and mysterious energy; it sometimes feels as though it is poised on the brink of another reality. And yet its liminality also overlaps with a world of prosaic modernity, with laybys and litter, luxurious country pads and solid 4G. Much like the season, this is a puckish in-between place, one of both darkness and light.

Penelope Lively's children's novel *The Whispering Knights*, partly inspired by the Rollrights, begins with a ritual of sorts. Three friends cook up a witchy brew in an old barn not too far from a collection of mysterious megaliths. Little do they know that their actions will summon the Arthurian enchantress Morgan le Fay to their quiet Cotswolds village. In the ensuing conflict with the witch, the stones will come to play a pivotal role.

The remains of a dolmen called the Whispering Knights stand on the site of the Rollright Stones, not far from the King's Men circle, and the folkloric origin story of these monuments is also one of witchcraft. In one of the most famous tales associated with megaliths, a mighty king and his army encounter a witch on her home turf, a hill above the village of

Long Compton. The witch announces to the king, "Seven long strides shalt thou take, and if Long Compton thou canst see, King of England thou shalt be!" For the king this is too easy, and he replies, "Stick, stock, stone, as king of England I shall be known!" He hasn't, however, clocked the earthen mound that can still be seen today beyond the solitary King Stone, and he fails in his task. The king, his men and the conspiratorial whispering knights (who perhaps know something of their master's hubris) are immediately turned to stone.

The tale of the Long Compton witch, as Carolyne Larrington notes, certainly "has something to say about masculine ambition and sense of entitlement, and about female resistance".[1] It also shows how this land was associated with the occult. The earliest references to the tale of the petrified army feature a Saxon general rather than a witch, but by the nineteenth century the sorceress was in place, perhaps as Long Compton and the surrounding area were increasingly associated with magical activity.

The antiquarian James Harvey Bloom gathered tales of Long Compton's witches in the early twentieth century: "The extreme south of Warwickshire was a stronghold of these creatures; they held their Sabbaths there, at the Rollright stones, a megalithic circle, to which green lanes converge along the hill tops." In Long Compton, Bloom tells us of a Mrs. F., who could "assume at will any form she chose to take", and of a young man who "sold himself to the evil one" and was provided with twelve imps in return.[2] Bloom relates other diabolical stories that he extracted from the village, all "seriously told, after much persuasion and with some fear of the consequences".[3] Popular belief in the dark arts may have been in decline, but not, it seemed, in the valley below the stones.

Perhaps the most notorious example of the fear of witches in Long Compton came in September 1875, when farm worker James Hayward brutally murdered the elderly Ann Tennant on his way home from the fields with his pitchfork, adamant that she had bewitched him. Hayward was obsessed with witches, blaming them for his various misfortunes and claiming upon his arrest that there were "fifteen more of them in the village that I will serve the same. I will kill them all." Unrepentant, he lived out his days in Broadmoor Asylum. A proverb that once circulated in the

Author Penelope Lively drew uncanny inspiration from the Rollrights

area ran, "There are enough witches in Long Compton to draw a wagon load of hay up Long Compton hill."[4] For Ann Tennant, like so many accused of witchcraft in the centuries before her, these old superstitions were twisted into a malevolent reality.

Long Compton recounts its folk tales and murderous occult links in the centre of the village with a colourfully illustrated information board (complete with sprouting foliate head and wizened witchy hand), and not far from here you can begin the climb up the hill towards the Rollrights.

The King's Stone, the petrified remains of an overly ambitious monarch

The path runs easily alongside salubrious renovations in yellow Cotswold stone; freshly installed fences and gates abound, while gardens fly the occasional Union Jack. Nonetheless, in autumn, with a chill wind in the air, the climb soon feels more effortful than it first looks. The witch was right; these hills can deceive.

Following the ascent, there's a fair bit of road walking to get to the site, and it pays to take a diversion through the picturesque village of Little

"The complex is entwined with fairies, witches and mysterious energy; it sometimes feels as though it is poised on the brink of another reality"

Rollright to beat the worst of it. The roadside can't be entirely avoided, however, and nor can its own peculiar archaeology: Costa cups, Space Raiders packets and an unopened can of hipster IPA, the latter placed thoughtfully on a fence like a lost hat or glove. The veil between one world and the next might be thin, but so is that between modernity and the ancient past.

Once you've popped a coin in the honesty box and you emerge through the trees into the complex proper, you are soon confronted not by the witch of Long Compton, but Robin Goodfellow – or at least a wicker figure of the same. The Rollright Trust, who manage the monuments, have installed several impressive wicker sculptures over the years, including a witch that loomed spectacularly above the King Stone and over the view of Long Compton below. All are the work of local artists David Gosling and his son Adam, and, when we visit, their current piece is particularly striking. Puck is striding towards the King's Men circle, one arm raised aloft and long, claw-like fingers seemingly engaged in either a curse or warning. Winged creatures throng his cloak, and the whole sculpture is somehow suggestive of a giant insect. Seen side on with the circle, its lurch towards the King's Men feels animate and faintly ominous. Shakespeare himself may have looked out on the stones on his way to and from Stratford along the ancient drover's road. However, this wicker creature is perhaps more reminiscent of Neil Gaiman's menacing

reading of Puck in *The Sandman* or the decadent fairies of Susanna Clarke's *Jonathan Strange & Mr Norrell* than the Bard's genial trickster.

Like all of the monuments on the site, the King's Men are composed of distinctive oolitic limestone that has, over the course of thousands of years, eroded to leave a wonderfully pockmarked, Swiss-cheese effect on the stones. (Perhaps, if left to weather and decay, the same will eventually happen to the limestone residences of Long Compton, down the hill.) There is a definite feeling of energy in the circle – dowsers report their rods frequently go bonkers among the stones and ley line hunters have tied the site to numerous possible alignments. But you don't have to dig deep into earth mysteries to engage with the sense that this monument, built in the late Neolithic and of sublime ritual significance for generations, is a potent place.

As you walk through the small copse that sits alongside the King's Men, tied ribbons, as seen at holy wells, speak to the continued sacred significance of the complex for many. And amid the colourful rags and bags of incense are more unusual offerings that again reveal the juxtaposition of present with past here – a plastic toy llama, a Vodafone lanyard ribbon. The present haunts the past in surprising ways. For while the folk tales may tell of witches and

imps, more recent rumours circulate of the Rollright Stones and their handy laybys as a venue for trading misappropriated vegetables from local farms, spuds no doubt enchanted by their proximity to the site's mysteries.

The Whispering Knights stand a short walk from the King's Men. Once the stones would have formed an impressive portal dolmen, constructed around 3800 BCE, but even in its dilapidated state the monument has its own special charm. It is also perfectly named; we've spent a good while sat admiring these strangely humanoid stones that seem to be carousing and colluding like old friends. At the side of the Knights, more woodland has been given over to assorted environmental artworks, including a log labyrinth and giant wicker structures that add to the sense of a visit to faerie, especially when the wind catches the fallen leaves in the wood.

In Penelope Lively's novel, the Rollrights are reimagined as the Hampden Stones, "gaunt guardians of the valley" that sit at the border of our world, charged with latent power. In the autumn twilight, the stones above Long Compton wear the weight of their lore lightly in a silence broken only by the occasional van on the road that runs too close to the site. The stones are at peace with their ambiguous, liminal status, content to wait out another few thousand years, while the lanyard hippies, potato pinchers, dowsers, witches and weird walkers continue to be drawn into their mysterious orbit.

WALKING NOTES

There is parking right outside the Rollrights in the form of a layby, but in the loose route above we began in Long Compton. As we note, there is some road walking, which isn't ideal, but can be mitigated somewhat by a route through the hamlet of Little Rollright (SP 29348 30133), which takes you past its ancient church and brings you out at the Whispering Knights (SP 29931 30840). Remember to donate some cash to the Rollright Trust, who look after this amazing place.

BLAKENEY POINT

A ghostly resonance at East Anglia's desolate edge

NORFOLK, ENGLAND (TG 02254 45959)
OS EXPLORER 251

F ew writers of ghost stories have summoned a sense of place like E. F. Benson. Though primarily known in his day as a novelist who satirised early-twentieth-century high society, his enduring "spook stories" revel in darker themes, and it was out here, at Norfolk's marshy northern edge, that one of Benson's most vivid hauntings would emerge.

Edward Frederic Benson was born into a remarkable, privileged Victorian family. His mother was renowned in society circles for her intelligence and wit, while his father, Edward White Benson, would eventually become Archbishop of Canterbury. The six Benson children all set out on their own paths: Egyptologist Margaret became the first woman to be granted permission to excavate in Egypt, while two of Edward's brothers would also become writers, publishing noted ghost stories of their own. The children retained a close connection to the Church after the death of their father – Robert Hugh Benson would become an Anglican priest before controversially converting to Catholicism. However, these ecclesiastical persuasions sat in sharp contrast to the family's unusual occult pedigree. The archbishop, for example, was a founding member of the Cambridge Ghost Society, which was devoted to an academic exploration of supernatural phenomena. More sinisterly, the children's grandfather

181

was a student of a Dr Sollitt of York, a chemist familiar with the dark arts, who believed he could summon the Devil himself.[1] The effect of one such summoning was a mighty *Poltergeist*-style disruption of furniture, which caused the doctor to burn his arcane texts and renounce magic for good.

There was light and dark in the Benson bones, and Edward himself would happily admit the irrational, recounting ghostly experiences at his house in Rye (purchased from Henry James, which must have turned up the spook vibe a notch) in a short essay, "The Secret Garden". A key thread within the writer's ghost stories is that of resonance. Events have a way of

"Benson's resonant ghosts are presences imprinted upon the landscape at significant moments, to be accessed, often fearfully and without warning, at a later date"

leaving a trace upon the surroundings within which they occur. In some tales, such as "The Bed by the Window", a violent act allows time itself to appear as a Mobius strip: the murder to come has already occurred and this future–past reverberates endlessly at the scene of the crime. As Benson suggests in "The Flint Knife", an unsettling tale of an unearthed "altar of sacrifice", some places "have their 'atmosphere' which has been distilled from the thoughts and the personalities of those who have inhabited them".[2] Houses and, indeed, landscapes remember.

Benson was drawn to marshes, and several of his most chilling tales occur in these sorts of weird surroundings, whether Romney Marsh near his home in Rye, or out in Norfolk, where he enjoyed birdwatching. "A Tale of an Empty House" was inspired by the uncanny desolation of

Blakeney Point and its Watch House. It is around this strange edifice that the story's phantom flickers. When the holidaying protagonist comes upon the house beyond the marshes, it seems "an unwarrantable invasion of the emptiness". He hears, and even glimpses, a man hobbling inside the place, although locals later inform him that the remote structure is uninhabited. On returning to the marshes, birdwatching with a friend, the two take shelter in the Watch House when a storm flares up. It is now that Benson ratchets up the tension, for "the lame man" soon returns to his property: "At that moment not fright, but fear, which is a very different matter, closed in on me." The events play out, and ghostly peril abounds. When the tale's narrator is safely back in London, he hears of a murder trial concerning a crime committed on Norfolk's marshes. In the dock was a lame man and his awful crime was committed in a disused coastguard house "in as lonely a place as you would find anywhere in England".[3]

The village of Blakeney is rendered as Riddington in Benson's tale, and the view that confronts the narrator when he wakes in his hotel remains largely as Benson describes. The marshes have also retained their reputation as a birdwatching mecca: folk can be seen lugging tripods and eye-wateringly expensive camera lenses throughout the year. Indeed, the birdlife-dedicated visitor centre in nearby Cley next the Sea is a good spot to begin a trek out to the Watch House.

Walking from Cley across the marshes is an easy-going ramble. The pools and dykes below the raised footpath allow opportunities to spot the brilliantly named black-tailed godwit, while the windmill and whitewashed houses of the village retreat behind you. Once the beach is finally reached, however, the wind picks up and the atmosphere changes. This is a place at the edge of things, and from the tractors and lobster pots at the end of the beach road, the walk to the Watch House begins along the shingle.

There are wrecks on this journey, both at sea and on land. The SS Vera lies beneath the waves, just over 100m (330ft) out from the beach, after running aground in 1914. Another boat rusts in scrubland on the way to the house, its body gradually being consumed by marsh grasses. Not far from this hulk, the remains of the medieval Blakeney Chapel are still marked on the OS map, although no ruins are now visible above ground. Benson's ghostly killer is not the only thing haunting this landscape.

Master of the
Norfolk spook
story, E. F. Benson

183

The sight of the Watch House in the far distance affirms Benson's impression of an incongruous presence in the bleak landscape, and the house still seems a way off after a significant effort. It can feel like you are walking for an age on shingle, especially as the surface gives the uncanny sensation of someone tracing your steps, as pebbles skitter and skip behind you with each pace. It is some relief when the path to the house is reached and the beach walking is over for a while.

Originally built to shelter coastguards on the lookout for smugglers, the Watch House is an unusual and evocative site, and it is easy to see why it excited such eerie thoughts in Benson's imagination. It would certainly be hard to imagine a more desolate spot. The blue painted door and window frames stand out boldly against the cloudy autumn sky, and large weathered timbers lie alongside the front of the house, studded with rusted iron fittings. In a nod to the house's haunted heritage, a crude skeleton has been daubed on the building's water tank, while an ornate candlestick has been left on the front step. Not far away, a wooden jetty allows access to the Watch House by boat. At low tide it looks out onto an expanse of mud flats and marsh, water pooling here and there.

Recently, it has been possible to rent the Watch House for an overnight stay. Benson toys with this thought himself in "A Tale of an Empty House". We can safely say he wouldn't be signing up, for, in his own words: "If from some unconjecturable cause one was forced to spend the night here, how the mind would long for any companionship, how sinister would become the calling of the birds, how weird the whistle of the wind round the cavern of this abandoned habitation."[4] What dreams will visit you in the Watch House we cannot say.

Benson's resonant ghosts are presences imprinted upon the landscape at significant moments, to be accessed, often fearfully and without warning, at a later date. His fiction aligns with what would come to be known as Stone Tape theory, popularised by the academic, explorer and parapsychologist T. C. Lethbridge in the 1960s.[5] Lethbridge proposed that ghosts could be explained as a kind of "tape recording", and this idea would be picked up by Nigel Kneale in his classic Christmas Day teleplay, *The Stone Tape*. Since its broadcast in 1972, the play has given its name to the idea that the natural and manmade environment can hold residual impressions of past events.

As Benson states in "The Secret Garden", describing his own paranormal experience, "It was as if something out of the past, some condition of life long vanished, was leaking through into the present."[6] Some ancient objects, also thought long vanished, have also been preserved in marshland due to the particular characteristics of this environment. Another Norfolk settlement, Holme-next-the-Sea, would give up the iconic Seahenge timber circles, originally built on marshland before erosion led them to the waves. The salty silt protected the wood and allowed archeologists to date the monuments with remarkable accuracy to 2049 BCE. Benson would no doubt have appreciated the connection between ancient memory and marshes. On this exposed section of the North Norfolk coast, especially in autumn, the haunted world, the world of revenant presences, can still leak through.

WALKING NOTES

Although it's possible to park at Cley Beach, we reckon it's a better walk from Cley Marshes Visitor Centre (TG 05401 44011). There are all the necessary amenities here, and you get to enjoy the contrasting wander through the marshland before hitting the shingle. Blakeney Watch House can be found at TG 02254 45959. The walk from the visitor centre to the Watch House is around 4.5km (2.8 miles). You can, of course, carry on from the Watch House to Blakeney Point and its famous seal colony.

OTTERY ST MARY

Autumn's anarchic spirit abounds in Devonshire

DEVON, ENGLAND (SY 09890 95563)
OS EXPLORER 115

One of the most spectacular and dangerous English customs takes place on 5 November in the Devon town of Ottery St Mary. Flaming tar barrels career around the streets, spitting fire into the autumn night. The barrels are carried by local men and women, who hoist up each inferno outside a sponsoring pub and leg it down the road, their mates jostling for the opportunity to take on the task. It's a raucous and awe-inspiring event that has the capacity to conjure up our primal association with fire.

The origins of the Ottery Tar Barrels are obscure, but almost certainly relate to the Guy Fawkes celebrations that developed across England in the seventeenth century. Once, blazing tar barrels featured in many events commemorating Parliament's near miss, and a similar custom is to be found in Hatherleigh, in the west of Devon, where lit barrels are pulled through the town on sledges. However, nothing comes near to the raw thrill of Ottery St Mary, where folk charge about with monstrous incendiaries within close proximity of a crowd. Health and safety rules do not seem to apply in this corner of Devon – the one concession to spectator welfare appears to have occurred in the Victorian period, with the banning of the option of rolling your flaming barrel down the street. Primary school age children take part

187

earlier in the evening, but they are given smaller barrels, still flaming of course.

The barrels ignite so forcefully due to a uniquely combustible Ottery combination of tar and paraffin. The carriers themselves have little in the way of protection (a rugby shirt and a pair of gloves seemingly does the trick) but there is a hard-won knack to the whole process, which means that injuries are rare. Skills are tested as the huge barrels are passed, with the casks eventually beginning to collapse in flames until the remains are thrown down to smoulder in the street. This is a moment of great delight for the crowd, and phones are held aloft as if documenting a real-ale fuelled pyrotechnic rave. It's a tradition that leaves its mark on all who witness it. Artist Ben Edge, whose folkloric paintings capture the spirit of so many customs, described to us the electricity in the air:

> As the evening progresses, the barrels grow in size and so does the danger. There are drunken teenagers lining the streets; the smell of singed hair, tar and burning clothes fills the atmosphere. My face becomes covered in tar and small blisters as I run by the barrel's side, trying to capture the action. For those taking part there is a seriousness, a deep respect for the ritual, and as the roaring midnight barrel finally burns out, there are tears in the eyes of young men who were given the honour of running with it for the first time. They have come full circle, and are now one of the elders.

Not just anyone can carry a barrel in this town, though. The writer Nick Groom notes that many of the same families have been running the barrels since the mid-nineteenth century and the rights to engage in this risky business are tightly controlled.[1] A distinct local pride echoes in this place far beyond the activities of the Fifth, with another unique (and more sedate) local custom, the midsummer Pixie Day, starting up as recently as the mid-twentieth century. The town even has a society of Ottery expats,

formed in the 1890s and known as the Old Ottregians. The church
bells play their theme tune, "The Ottery Song", daily:

> There is a place, dear native place!
> Amid the meadows fair,
> Between the hills, beside the stream,
> Where blows the soft light air.
> O! Ottery dear! O! Ottery fair!
> The West! The West for me!

The Old Ottregians are not unique in their devotion to a fire festival,
however. Although there is no direct link to the festival of Samhain
that would have taken place around this time of year, a similar vibe
is certainly channelled at Ottery. Little is known about the original
observances at the Gaelic forerunner of the modern Halloween,
but what is clear is that Samhain was a time of divination, when
supernatural forces were abroad. It makes sense that people in a
precarious world would choose this point of the year to ask their
ancestors, or their gods, what their future would hold and, perhaps,
who would make it through the cold days to come. As late as the
eighteenth century, writers reported the use of stones to divine fates
next to the Scottish Samhain bonfire:

> On All Saints' Even they set up bonfires in every village.
> When the bonfire is consumed, the ashes are carefully
> collected into the form of a circle. There is a stone put in near
> the circumference, for every person of the several families
> interested in the bonfire; and whatever stone is removed out
> of its place or injured before the next morning, the person
> represented by that stone is devoted, or fey, and is supposed
> not to live twelve months from that day . . .[2]

Stories of fairies, goblins and other supernatural creatures having
to be avoided, or even propitiated, at this time are widespread
across British folklore, remnants perhaps of a prehistoric belief in

189

"It makes sense that people in a precarious world would choose this point of the year to ask their ancestors, or their gods, what their future would hold and, perhaps, who would make it through the cold days to come"

a post-harvest supernatural threat at Samhain. Interestingly, it is only with the arrival of Christianity and the development of Hallowtide (which incorporates Halloween, All Hallows' and All Souls' Day) that the intensifying aspect of the remembrance of the dead seems to have been introduced, fusing with Samhain's existing uncanny vibrations and laying a path towards the modern Halloween.[3]

At Ottery, the daring, contest-like spirit of the Tar Barrels, alongside the roar of the bonfire and the funfair's howls, suggest a Devonshire take on the ancient Gaelic celebrations, which have enjoyed a revival in recent years. The flames rushing through the crowd in the chill autumn air connects to something fundamental within us – some ancestral memory of fire, the element that in many ways made us who we are, perhaps being involved in the development of consciousness itself.

Fire's strange properties, its capacity to produce calm, meditative states and its occasional raging ferocity, would have captivated early human minds. In his remarkable *Being a Human*, Charles Foster suggests that "no dramatic out-of-body experience is needed for the kindling of consciousness. Lots of staring into a fire will do instead."[4] Fire would certainly have seemed an enchanted element back in deep time, but if the control of fire did ignite something within us, then we can all still sense its importance. It is there in the visceral excitement of Ottery's tar barrel runs, and the hypnotic flicker of its bonfire's flames. Just as we give thanks to the sun, especially in this season, we also acknowledge the power of fire.

A flaming good time at the 1973 event

WALKING NOTES

During the Tar Barrels event, Ottery is closed to traffic, but some parking is available on the edge of town. Details can be found on the event website, which also contains safety guidelines for spectators. As mentioned, Ottery's other festival is Pixie Day. The event commemorates the legend that the local pixies, so enraged by the ringing of church bells, kidnapped the town's bell ringers and kept them in a cave (still known as Pixie's Parlour). The bell ringers' capture and subsequent escape have been re-enacted by Ottregians annually since 1954.

THE DEVIL'S QUOITS

An unlikely path to re-enchantment is unveiled

OXFORDSHIRE, ENGLAND (SP 41116 04757)
OS EXPLORER 180

The Devil's Den, Chair, Arrows – many of our most captivating and numinous megalithic sites have been afflicted with a demonic prefix. After the Church let the Devil loose in Britain, he was added to folklore's list of supernatural beings capable of shaping the landscape and creating monuments seemingly beyond mortal skill. The Devil's presence at prehistoric sites is a complex one, however, which extends beyond phenomenal feats of strength. Satan could also be co-opted to reinforce Church teaching, especially after the Reformation, by turning various blasphemous hedonists into stone (see Stanton Drew, page 93). And although Beelzebub's entry into the folkloric monument building trade has been shown to be a fairly late one, he was incredibly successful in England especially, putting the likes of giants and elves out of business.[1] In the satanic overtones that reverberate in his work, we can still glimpse negative or fearful connotations. Perhaps, then, the time is right for a mass rededication of our devilish megaliths – to recharge these sites with auspicious titles befitting their positive energies.

The lore that surrounds the Devil's Quoits, near the village of Stanton Harcourt in Oxfordshire, sees Satan engaging in his usual chucking competition; this time with an unlucky beggar who loses

193

his soul when the fiend decides to start flinging some serious stones around to win the game. Unlike the fairly standard folk account of its origins, the site itself is wonderful and curious in many ways.

Access to the Devil's Quoits is from a dump of the kind we are now told is a recycling centre, a trackway running the fringe of a man-made lake to reach the stones. This is a world of gravel extraction

"The functional and the sacred, the ancient and the modern, collide in surreal fashion on the edge of Stanton Harcourt"

and semi-rural waste management, where the occasional fencepost is cryptically spray-painted blue, and signs inform you of assembly points and active landfill. It is also, like many of these edgeland places, a haven for wildlife and possessed of an unusual calm – aside from the occasional dog walker or birder, few folk seem to frequent these paths.

When the stones emerge from beyond recently planted trees, they are a beautiful sight, alternating between rusty oranges and bold greys. This is a classic henge, with a bank and ditch encircling the formidable megaliths. Large uprights stand at the circle's entrances and a solitary stone lies off-circle, hinting at some kind of solar alignment. The shadows that spill from the stones are juxtaposed with those from nearby plant machinery, the landfill site butting up against the ceremonial landscape, its strange artificial hillsides looming over the henge's earthworks. The functional and the sacred, the ancient and the modern, collide in surreal fashion on the edge of Stanton Harcourt.

Not so long ago, the henge was a shadow of its former self. The gravel works, farming and even RAF runway construction all had a hand in the decline of the original monument, and by 1940 only one stone was standing here. A bold reconstruction project by a collection of agencies was begun in the first decade of this century to return the circle to something close to how it looked in its heyday. A clear map of the complex's phases was obtained from the archaeology, and the remaining original uprights (found buried in the ditch or elsewhere) were re-erected. The many missing stones were replaced with choice conglomerate rock from nearby Ducklington, lending the site its varying megalithic hues as ancient stone mixes with newly quarried blocks. The ditch and bank were also restored, so that the site was in a similar condition to when the Romans would have first laid eyes on it almost two thousand years ago.

Such restoration has its detractors, of course. Yet any purists yearning for ruinous authenticity are missing the point with the Devil's Quoits. In the shadow of so much modern utility, a ritual landscape has returned courtesy of a waste recycling company and the local council. Perhaps the Quoits offer up an idea of what could be achieved in new builds across the land, not through restoration, but in a bold new sacred and pluralistic vision – the return of stone circles to the landscape. When every fresh estate has its own stone circle, maybe we can look into some truly propitious names for these sites that leave the Devil behind and acknowledge our deep psychic connection to this ancient land.

WALKING NOTES

There is parking for the Devil's Quoits at SP 40853 04466 and the circle is crudely signposted from this point. Follow the path that runs alongside the lake to reach the stones.

There are several other interesting sites further north, including the magnificent Hawk Stone at SP 33935 23544, some 30km (18.6 miles) away from the Quoits. The Rollright Stones (see page 172) can be found 12km (7.5 miles) north of the Hawk Stone.

DOLL TOR

Humanity's complex relationship with the old stones

DERBYSHIRE, ENGLAND (SK 23833 62865)
OS EXPLORER OL24

Stanton Moor is an extraordinary place. Within this small stretch of the Peak District the geology of Millstone Grit has conspired to create amazing natural pillars of rock, while the same stone has been wrought by human hands in monuments such as the elegant Nine Ladies circle. Few places in Britain have seen such an interaction between man and megalith. Witness the eighteenth-century carved features of Rowtor Rocks behind the Druid Inn in the village of Birchover, or the Victorian footholds chipped into the massive outcrops of the Cork and Andle Stones – only the latest marks on rock that has held prehistoric indentations for millennia. The interplay between humans and the landscape has seemingly always been enacted on the moor. And perhaps one little-known site tells this tale best of all.

There is something about the siting of ancient monuments within woodland that allows for a deeply evocative experience. Much like Aberdeenshire's tree-shrouded Sunhoney or the Welsh chambered tomb of Gwal-y-filiast, the small Doll Tor circle is much enhanced by its foliate setting. Tucked away on private land, and requiring permission to visit, the circle has a distinctly unassuming nature. None of its uprights stand taller than 1m (3ft) and the circle itself is

199

"When we are barred from the land we do not develop this meaningful connection, which makes acts of vandalism – such as that at Doll Tor – far more likely to occur"

only 6m (19.7ft) across. Nonetheless, there is a remarkably peaceful, powerful ambience in this place. Others clearly feel it too, with offerings of berries, feathers and carefully wound twigs adorning a nearby tree and one of the stones. A ring of pine cones lies at the circle's centre. It's a tranquil scene, but such calm hides a turbulent modern history.

Doll Tor was erected in the Bronze Age and, at some point, a small accompanying cairn was added at its eastern edge, now scattered with ferns and the occasional impressive mushroom. The monument doubtless contentedly lived out most of its existence without much human interference, especially after the rituals that were once performed here had passed into memory. However, its recent story tells us a great deal about our ongoing and complex relationship with ancient monuments. Like many sites, Doll Tor was investigated by a Victorian antiquarian, in this case the wealthy "barrow knight" Thomas Bateman. Further excavations were carried out in the 1930s, as a commemorative stone on the site attests, and it was during this period that three uprights were somehow broken up in mysterious circumstances, leaving the excavators to cement the stones back together.

Doll Tor would even hit the headlines in 1993 when someone bizarrely took it upon themselves to "restore" the circle by re-erecting stones and filling in presumed gaps with new uprights. The number of stones more than doubled, from six to fourteen. As a result of this surprise makeover, English Heritage financed another restoration to return Doll Tor to its prehistoric appearance, and all seemed well in the woods, for a while at least.

Few people are as connected to the prehistoric monuments of these isles as Sam Grimshaw, whose Instagram feed is a treasure trove of megalithic content. Sam is a relentless documentarian of ancient sites and has long felt a connection to Doll Tor, rightly noting the "heavy ancient feeling" the place conjures. In 2020, as the UK's first COVID-19 lockdown eased, evidence of the latest incident in Doll Tor's unfortunate history emerged. The monument had been vandalised and fires lit around the circle, with stones being used for seating and even in a fire pit. It was Sam who discovered the vandalism, as he explained to us:

> Doll Tor is a cairn circle, and there's still plenty of cairn stones strewn around the monument. Many of the stones had been removed to build the fire pit, leaving large sockets everywhere; they had been cracked into several pieces from the heat. A second fire was built into the wall of the cairn, which also left a mess, burned the grass and cracked the stones. On top of this, a large boulder had been dragged from the forest and used as a bench. The place was a mess – I've never seen anything so disrespectful at an ancient site before.

Over the centuries, people's attitudes to monuments have veered between indifference, reverence and downright contempt. Doll Tor's story reminds us that it is naïve to think that excessive disregard for sites has been consigned to history. If we are to reap the benefits of a reconnection with our ancient landscape, we must find a way to ensure that its most valuable places are held close to all our hearts. There is perhaps no better spot to do this than up on Stanton Moor, where

Rowtor Rocks: part folly, part cave complex at nearby Birchover

humans and megaliths have been entwined from time immemorial. As Sam states, "I think educating people about how important and fragile these places are is a big must." This idea resonates with the right to roam movement, who believe that increasing access to the natural world is the first step to creating a bond with nature, which in turn leads to a sense of responsibility for it. When we are barred from the land we do not develop this meaningful connection, which makes acts of vandalism – such as that at Doll Tor – far more likely to occur.

A hopeful note was sounded across the moor not long ago, at the Nine Ladies stone circle, where a lengthy campaign took place to prevent nearby quarry sites being reopened and the inevitable degradation of the area. The protestors were eventually successful, and the permission to quarry was revoked. It's a powerful thing when people unite, not to damage these sacred spaces, but to save them.

WALKING NOTES

Doll Tor is on private land and permission should be sought from the landowner before visiting. There is a disused quarry beyond the circle, so avoid this area for safety reasons.

The impressive natural pillar of the Cork Stone can be seen at SK 24341 62785. The Nine Ladies stone circle is around 1km (0.6 mile) from the Cork Stone at SK 24912 63493.

The Druid Inn is located in Birchover and serves a cracking pint. Behind the pub, the sprawling Rowtor Rocks are a must for exploration. Here, genuine prehistoric rock art mingles with caves, tunnels, steps and even a "throne" carved at the behest of Thomas Eyre, an eccentric reverend who died in 1717. It's a twisting, turning place with some big drops, so mind how you go.

FERNWORTHY FOREST

An atmospheric gateway to Dartmoor's megalithic treasure trove

DEVON, ENGLAND (SX 66096 82641)
OS EXPLORER OL28

Dartmoor is a weird place; temporal dislocation comes with the territory. Wayfinding is not easy among this gorse, these rambling tors and secluded brooks. And when an autumn mist descends, you can be transported: a Bronze Age farmer to your left, a medieval tin miner to your right, and up ahead the lord of the manor has antiquarian ambitions. He's just repositioned those stones. The earth gnomes don't approve.

The stretch of moor between the storied Warren House Inn and the foreboding interwar plantation of Fernworthy Forest is classic Dartmoor; the grasses are thick underfoot and marshy ground emerges without warning, saturated by the capricious weather. Long ago, the moorland here would have rolled uninterrupted and Fernworthy's ancient monuments would have been as exposed as their neighbours at Merrivale or the Grey Wethers. Now, the break with the moor is absolute, and dark evergreens offer up an entrance out of a Grimm's tale. Once inside, the silent monoculture can provide even the warmest October day with an eerie chill.

Near the edge of the forest sits Assycombe double stone row, Fernworthy's planters helpfully leaving a gap between the saplings for the stones to breathe. Although little known, it is a remarkable monument

that seems to tumble down its grassy hill, the irregular miniliths descending like a dragon's spine from an initial menhir to a large blocking stone at the foot of the slope.

Assycombe is one of the many stone rows on Dartmoor thought by early antiquarians, such as Richard Polwhele, to be "Druid ways". They are scattered across the landscape, sometimes barely discernible, but always potent in their imaginative value. Walking these ancient lines creates an access point, a connection to those who walked them long ago.

"Once inside, the silent monoculture can provide even the warmest October day with an eerie chill"

Following the track from Assycombe, deeper into the plantation, will eventually bring you to the reservoir that dominates the area. Built during the Second World War, its construction was not without incident. Fernworthy Farm, which could trace its ancestry back to the Middle Ages, was among the buildings demolished to make way for the dam and reservoir. When it was standing, locals told of a curse laid upon the farm by the earth gnomes who dwell beneath the moor. So infuriated were the gnomes by the quarrying of their finest granite to rebuild the farmhouse at Fernworthy, they stole the firstborn of the farmer who'd committed the sin. Much later, the gnomes were also blamed by some for the horrendous storm that delayed the construction of the dam, covering the reservoir's construction site with silt and washing away a crane in the process. On Dartmoor, "don't upset the gnomes" seems to be pretty high up the list of folk rules.[1]

Working around the body of water as it lies today, it's an easy stroll to the mysterious stone circle of Froggymead, its name nodding to its marshy location. A Bronze Age circle of some twenty-nine stones, it is a wonderfully meditative place. Stone rows, albeit damaged by all that tree planting, can be seen to the north and south of the site. Froggymead (also known as Fernworthy stone circle) makes a vibe-laden picnic spot and, from here, there's the option to continue out of the forest to the Grey Wethers.

Consisting of two stunning stone circles, the Grey Wethers are one of the megalithic highlights of this part of the world. Their position makes them even more appealing – you're likely to be sharing the circles with relatively few visitors or perhaps only the skylarks that dance overhead. Writing in the eighteenth century, Polwhele noted that Dartmoor, with its "druidical scenery" and natural wonders "hath the effect of enchantment".[2] With Sittaford Tor looming alongside the old stones, this site is a case in point.

The Grey Wethers are also dripping with local lore. Their very name is linked to the story of a drunken farmer who was tricked into buying the stones as a flock of sheep ("wether" meaning male sheep, from the Old English *weðer*). Another tale tells that on Midsummer Eve, at midnight, the stones magically transform into rams, and that catching and shearing one will yield a golden fleece.

From the Grey Wethers, you can head back through the forest for a pint at the Warren House Inn: a fine place to wind up after a day's yomping. Its fire has been burning solidly since the current building was put up in 1845 and, as one of the highest and most isolated pubs in England, visitors have often welcomed the warmth, especially when autumn arrives. Indeed, it has always been tempting to stop here, as a sign recorded outside the pub in the 1830s made clear:

> Here is cider and beer,
> Your hearts for to cheer.
> And if you want meat
> To make up a treat,
> There are rabbits to eat.

The plentiful rabbits were no doubt taken from the nearby warrens mentioned in the pub's name, and a particularly folkloric motif of three rabbits chasing each other appears on the current sign.

The inn has its share of tales that have been told around the fire for many years, a favourite being "The Salted Corpse". This yarn tells of a traveller staying overnight who opens up an intriguing chest in his room. To his horror, he finds himself gazing upon the face of a dead man. Suspecting murder, he rushes to the landlord, who casually informs him that "'tis only father", the old man having been salted down and stored until the trip can be made from the remote inn to Lydford for burial.[3]

Dartmoor is not as out of the way as it once was, and we would hope that there is less need to reach for the salt cellar these days. However, this land has somehow managed to retain a peculiar flavour of isolation well into the twenty-first century, and, especially away from its most-frequented spots, it still holds almost limitless possibilities for exploration.

WALKING NOTES

This is actually a very weird route, but we liked it. (There are other, more straightforward, walks out there on the internet.) There are several parking spots near the Warren House Inn (SX 67423 80944) and from here we made our way across the moor to Fernworthy Forest. As with any moorland walking, this is a map and compass job, best done with pals and all the requisite gear. We entered the forest at SX 66068 81902. Assycombe stone row can be found at SX 66096 82641. From here, you can walk through the forest, skirting the reservoir, to Froggymead at SX 65486 84127. The walk can be extended out of the trees to the Grey Wethers at SX 63869 83134.

While you're in the neighbourhood, Bennett's Cross stands about 1km (0.6 miles) from the Warren House Inn (SX 67999 81626), one of a number of ancient stone crosses in the area. This one is an unusual example; the more you look, the more it appears to be writhing in agony. This hasn't deterred folk from trying to nick it, though, and a microchip is now neatly embedded in the granite should anybody attempt to make off with it again. The nearby Bronze Age settlement of Grimspound (SX 70051 80904) is a 3.5km (2.2 miles) walk across the moor from the Warren House Inn (or a short drive) and is highly recommended. Absolutely rife with vibes.

WINTER

If the sun is the sublime charge that powers our seasons, then now it is at its weakest, its lowest ebb.

For our ancestors, winter could be a precarious time – prehistoric hunters would find their prey limited; medieval farmers would need to draw upon reserves of salted and smoked meat. And, perhaps most of all, this was a season of darkness, of short days with no electricity to replicate the sun's heat and light – a time of hunkering down and reflecting upon the year and, perhaps, those who had passed over. Across the centuries, people have both warded off and communed with this winter darkness and all that it encompasses: the unknown, the supernatural, death.

The shortest day of all belongs to the Neolithic statement monument, Stonehenge. Here, we can see the lines drawn between the living and the dead within a landscape linked to Britain's story from time immemorial. In the Scottish town of Burghead, over 900km (560 miles) north of Stonehenge, fires still usher in the New Year, while on the Welsh border with England, the ancient tradition of wassailing is combined with the ghostly custom of the Mari Lwyd. This is a time of uncanny celebration, when links to the past are at their most pronounced.

Wandering out in this season, we approach something of its mystery. It is there in Silbury Hill and the ancient sites that scatter its vicinity. We can feel it in the slow decline of Dunwich, out on an East Anglian coast beloved of one of the greatest writers of ghost stories (ideally told in winter, of course). It can be glimpsed in the mythic Peak District chasm of Lud's Church, where once, so the tale goes, Sir Gawain faced his verdant judge. Spring and rebirth lie ahead but, for now, we reckon with darkness.

SELECTED WINTER OBSERVANCES:
· Glastonbury Holy Thorn Cutting — mid-December
· Flamborough Sword Dance — Boxing Day
· Keynsham Mummers' Play — Boxing Day
· Allendale Tar Barrels — New Year's Eve
· Haxey Hood — 6 January (unless 6th is a Sunday)
· Llandysul Calan Hen — closest Saturday to 12 January
· Stroud Wassail — second Saturday in January
· Whittlesea Straw Bear Festival — weekend in January
· Lerwick Up Helly Aa — last Tuesday in January
· Alnwick Football — Shrove Tuesday

DUNWICH

In search of Britain's haunted Atlantis

SUFFOLK, ENGLAND (TM 47474 70602)
OS EXPLORER 231

Dunwich is one of Britain's most iconic lost places. The Suffolk port was once an international trading hub that supported around 4,000 souls within its bounds. However, coastal erosion and a series of catastrophic storms would put pay to the medieval city's expansion. A gradual but intermittently violent reclamation by the waves, beginning in the thirteenth century, resulted in much of the port being lost by the end of the Tudor period; at times buildings literally tumbled beneath the waves, giving the area the tabloid nickname of Britain's Atlantis. This much is well documented by those who have, over the centuries, become enchanted by this remnant village. Nevertheless, the Dunwich story continues to captivate and inspire, perhaps because of what it symbolises: Dunwich lays bare humanity's impermanence and the awesome, indifferent power of nature. A connection to these ideas is intensified in winter, when the North Sea smashes into Dunwich Beach with raucous vehemence and the sightseers are thin on the ground. It is in winter that the ghosts of the eastern shore are most alive.

Once through the relatively recent Forestry Commission plantation of Dunwich Forest, the village reveals itself as a small collection of buildings sheltering before the vast expanse of the North Sea. The water is often rough at this time of year, although it would have to go some way to top the storm that began on New Year's Eve 1286 and raged into 1287, one of several disastrous

tempests that ate away at Dunwich's land and eventually led to its almost complete desertion. Today, the beach café is about level with the medieval city's western edge. Everything east of here – the guildhall, the churches, the market, the alehouses and even the windmill – has incrementally fallen into the sea.

Dunwich Beach itself is dense with shingle and pebbles. Each rush of retreating waves shifts multicoloured stones, and the shingle banks tempt a hunt for quartz, hag stones and smooth, sea-worn glass. Storms can bring whole uprooted trees to the shoreline to lie prone beneath the cliffs that tower over the water. The shoreline is at once an idyllic and bleak spot, but perhaps the best place to wander upon arriving. The sea, after all, is the antagonist in this narrative (although some locals will tell you over a pint that Sizewell, the nuclear power station visible from the beach, is a far greater worry).

Perhaps the most famous legend associated with Dunwich is that of its bells. It is said that if you find yourself alone at high tide on the beach, the bells of the sunken churches can still be heard ringing out from the depths. It is this tale that inspired local acid folk luminaries Stone Angel to conjure "The Bells of Dunwich" for their self-titled 1975 LP, an album that draws upon the band's native landscape and lore. This gem of a release has gradually accrued a cult following since it was recorded, in pitch-perfect seventies manner, in an East Anglian teacher training college. "The Bells of Dunwich" is a forceful blend of flute, ringing acoustics and psychedelic spirals of lead guitar. Recently, one of the original 350 albums on the band's own Seashell label sold for £1,600 on Discogs, much to the bemusement of Stone Angel themselves, who still gig and record, continuing to channel local legend in their work.

Suffolk lad Brian Eno would take a more opaque approach when representing Dunwich Beach on 1982's *Ambient 4: On Land*. The album aims to transport the listener to a range of landscapes and has a distinctly East Anglian focus, with Leeks Hills near Woodbridge and Lantern Marsh (the Suffolk location of the top secret Cobra Mist radar project) also being referenced. Eno's drifting "Dunwich Beach, Autumn, 1960" is the album's final track. Winding back our seasonal clock from winter, the piece captures a strange, glacial tension in its delayed harmonics and shimmering drones. The spectre of Sizewell is perhaps present here as well – the contract to build the plant was signed off in the autumn of 1960, with all the optimism of the nuclear age, before construction began in the spring of the following year. Eno transports us to one of the last moments before the power station began to emerge, forever altering this landscape.

Away from the beach, an easy climb takes you towards the ruins of Greyfriars Friary. As you follow the footpath, it is easy to miss what is perhaps Dunwich's most affecting monument. On the cliff top, just a spit away from the edge, stands the last remaining grave of the churchyard of All Saints', the final ancient Dunwich church to collapse over the cliffs. The headstone is a simple inscription for Jacob Forster, who died in 1796 at only thirty-eight years of age. It is All Saints' Church that tangentially ties Dunwich to the work of the twentieth century's finest writer of ghost stories, M. R. James. In James's 1904 tale "Oh, Whistle, and I'll Come to You, My Lad", Parkins, a Cambridge professor holidaying in Suffolk, digs within the grounds of a Knights Templar preceptory, where he unearths an unusual bronze whistle. Following the find, the professor begins to notice a figure that appears to be tracking him. This doesn't deter him from inspecting the whistle back at his lodgings, where he finds it bears the vague and yet chillingly prophetic inscription, "QUIS EST ISTE

QUI UENIT" – "Who is this who is coming?" Out of curiosity, Parkins blows the whistle. From this point on the indistinct apparition the professor has glimpsed becomes increasingly threatening, both in dreams and terrifying reality.

"Oh, Whistle, and I'll Come to You, My Lad" is perhaps M. R. James's most masterful realisation of ancient dread, and it would receive a classic television adaptation at the hands of Jonathan Miller in 1968. Miller chose the graveyard of All Saints' as the location of the whistle's discovery by Michael Hordern, who portrayed the subtly renamed Professor Parkin. Even in the 1960s the site was more substantial than now – another headstone, that of John Brinkley Easey, would be lost over the cliffs in 1990. Dunwich's disappearing clifftop graveyard was the perfect backdrop to the professor's cursed discovery.

Hauntological pioneer Mark Fisher made a clear link between Miller's television adaptation on the cliffs above and Eno's *On Land* at the beach

"Dunwich lays bare humanity's impermanence and the awesome, indifferent power of nature"

below: "both in effect are meditations on the eerie as it manifested in the East Anglian terrain. With its lingering concentration on the landscape, its brooding silences, and its long scenes devoid of much action, it was as if Miller produced something like the television equivalent of the ambient music that Eno would later invent."[1] Ruminating on how he was able to sonically evoke both places he had actually visited and those he imagined visiting, Eno himself was distinctly hauntological in his sleeve notes to *On Land*, stating, "We feel affinities not only with the past, but also with the futures that didn't materialize." Dunwich's future may have been cancelled by the remorseless action of the sea, but it could certainly have enjoyed a different fate as a successful and enduring Suffolk port, had meteorology conspired differently.

Moving on from the spectral remains of All Saints' to Greyfriars Friary, the first thing you note is that, in a place defined by absence, there is a lot more left of this complex than others. Impressive walls and ornate arches suggest

219

something of the scale of the monastic compound. Even this, however, was a second go for the friars – their first site was damaged in that epic New Year's Eve storm of 1286. The friary ruins are estimated to have eighty years remaining before they too succumb to the sea.[2] Past the friary lies Greyfriars Wood, its holy triumvirate of oak, ash and thorn looking out over the sea. In the barren winter months, when the waves can be discerned between the trees, there is something wondrous about walking in woodland so close to the water, and we are reminded that Dunwich's original seaside wood, the Eastwood Forest, was one of the first stretches of land to be lost in the medieval period.

After passing through the woodland, you can hook a right along the country lanes for a wander back into the village and past the current Dunwich parish church. St James' Church was built on the grounds of the old leper hospital in 1832. Such institutions were constructed outside city walls and so it is telling as to how far Dunwich had receded by this point. The ruins of the leper hospital's chapel still stand on the site, but the real draw is the last buttress of All Saints' Church, rescued at great effort to stand in the new churchyard as a reminder of Dunwich's ecclesiastical past.

Not far from the new church, and alongside Dunwich's pub, the Ship, sits the museum. Although there have been some concessions to the twenty-first century, Dunwich Museum, with its blackboard informing visitors of erratic

opening hours, is a time capsule in itself, and all the better for it. In fact, the whole establishment would be well placed in a seventies children's folk horror (you know the type), with concerned kids bicycling across the village to eagerly consult the curator about an unfolding mystery.

Henry James wrote of Dunwich that "there is a presence in what is missing".[3] It is, in this sense, a deeply haunted place. But Dunwich also haunts us. Even by the time of the early antiquarians, the settlement was perceived as an archetypal place of ruins that had the capacity to hold a mirror to our own mortality. As the historian Matthew Green notes when discussing the antiquarians' take on Dunwich, "Ruins were memento mori par excellence; and none more so than ruins that were about to fall into the sea."[4] Something of this lingers in Dunwich as it survives today – it is one of Britain's truly hauntological locations. The city beneath the waves calls to us still.

WALKING NOTES

There is extensive parking at Dunwich Beach and this makes a good base for a walk around the area described above. The last grave (TM 47846 70368) can be seen before turning to visit the ruins of Greyfriars. Follow the footpath through Greyfriars Wood before eventually taking a path at TM 47476 70108 to head back in the direction of the village (with some road walking). On the site of St James' Church you will find the remains of the old leper hospital and the last buttress of All Saints' (TM 47474 70602).

If you fancy a longer ramble, there is a classic circular between two fine local pubs, the Westleton Crown and the Ship at Dunwich, taking in the dramatic vistas of Dunwich Heath. Map and details on the Westleton Crown website.

THE DEVIL'S ARROWS

Three massive stones among encroaching modernity

NORTH YORKSHIRE, ENGLAND (SE 39174 66491)
OS EXPLORER 299

In the megalithic Top Trumps stakes, Britain boasts some real worldies. At nearly 8m (26ft), the imposing Rudston Monolith is the tallest menhir in the country, standing proud in a Yorkshire churchyard; while in mass terms, the back stone of the cove at Avebury weighs in at a crushing 100 tonnes. These mind-blowing numbers are all the more remarkable when you consider the technology at the disposal of the prehistoric engineers. Using wooden stakes, antler picks and improvised rope, truly they were masters of their craft.

No less impressive than either of the standers mentioned above are the Devil's Arrows, found on the edge of Boroughbridge in North Yorkshire. There are three stones in this row, which today runs for over 170m (186yd). The stones decrease in height from south to north, with the southernmost stone being second only to the Rudston Monolith in height, clocking in at just under 7m (23ft). Four, or even five, stones once stood in the row, the missing menhirs falling victim to toppling by treasure hunters and bridge builders. The stones that remain, however, do not disappoint.

Getting up close to any of these monsters reveals the remarkable weathering that has taken place over the thousands of years since

they were erected. Deep grooves cascade down the stones, lending them a sculptural quality. No wonder the monument has exerted an influence on visiting artists, recently including Emii Alrai, who noted their "eerie and incredible" appearance.[1] We definitely concur on the stones' uncanny nature. On a winter's afternoon they present as Boroughbridge's silent guardians, towering enigmas shaded by leafless trees or standing tall in barren fields. What must they have seen in their millennia of solitude?

Solitude is perhaps being eroded as much as the stones themselves nowadays, with the site of the Devil's Arrows becoming a textbook juxtaposition of ancient and modern. Like some kind of folk horror plot point, the massive megaliths now stand at the entrance to a "collection" of new build houses (as the building firm, Linden Homes,

Not pictured: the incessant low rumble of nearby motorway traffic

"Deep grooves cascade down the stones, lending them a sculptural quality. No wonder the monument has exerted an influence on visiting artists"

styles it). These are stones for whom the landscape of the ancestors is now practically non-existent. Two have stood on cultivated land from time immemorial, and the tallest stone has been separated by a road and hedgerow for hundreds of years. More recently, the ceaseless hum of the A1(M) has been introduced, itself following an ancient trading route that was later taken up by the Romans.

The building of further houses edges the contemporary world even closer to these watchers of countless aeons. On our last visit, huge signs proclaimed "Last chance TO BUY", while a road called Chestnut Drive passed alongside new parking spaces for the Arrows. Other additions included an (admittedly useful) information board and a parade of Linden Homes banners. Perhaps the stones recall the legionaries who once passed this way, and draw some nostalgia from the billowing flags on the edge of their field. Another, even less welcome sign offers up a weak claim of legal action against those who dare cross the field to see the two stones found on private farmland.

All this juxtaposition of the numinous and mundane, home ownership and stone ownership, is enough to put you in a spin at this site. It is certainly nothing new for wondrous megaliths to be slammed up against modernity and, much as we love the wild, remote places, such contrasts can be

225

fascinating. There is, however, a definite melancholy about the way the Devil's Arrows and their land have been nibbled away by encroaching building projects, especially over the last hundred years. Yet, despite all this, the stone row still stands, enigmatic, inscrutable and even more worthy of a visit in these times of change. Although nobody can know how this landscape will evolve in the millennia to come, we would bet that the stones will be a constant, keeping watch, keeping guard.

WALKING NOTES

As we note above, access to the Devil's Arrows has been (somewhat ironically) improved with the arrival of the new houses. An information board and dedicated parking is now provided at SE 39174 66491. The southernmost and tallest stone can be found in its own accessible area at SE 39145 66438. The two slightly smaller stones in the row are on private land.

The site's traditional folklore states that an angry Devil targeted his arrows at nearby Aldborough, for reasons unknown. His fiendish aim was not true and the stones landed close to Boroughbridge instead. Another, more inventive, tale tells of a Druid who was fed up of having his crops pinched by local ne'er-do-wells and so made a pact with the Devil to ensure he would be pillaged no more. Upon the thieves' next attempt, Satan unleashed his terrible arrows and the Druid was never bothered again (although he did now have three massive stones on his land).

STONEHENGE

The world's preeminent pagan temple at its midwinter peak

WILTSHIRE, ENGLAND (SU 12240 42185)
OS EXPLORER 130 (STONEHENGE), OL35 (WAUN MAWN),
157 (WEST WOODS)

T here was once a circle of stones on the island of Ireland known as the Giants' Dance. For millennia it stood atop the mountain Killaraus, having been brought to this spot by titanic folk from the shores of distant Africa. In the words of the wizard Merlin, these were "mystical stones and of a medicinal virtue". Merlin stated that the African giants who set down the megaliths would use them to cure ailments by bathing in water that had washed the stones. When special herbs were added to the enchanted liquid, battle wounds would miraculously close.

Merlin told the tale of the Giants' Dance to the British king Aurelius Ambrosius, who was eager to erect a monument to the Britons who had fallen fighting off Saxon invaders. And it was Merlin who suggested that the circle could be transported across the Irish Sea: "They are stones of a vast magnitude and wonderful quality; and if they can be placed here, as they are there, round this spot of ground, they will stand forever," he announced prophetically. The king was convinced and resolved to have them taken from the Irish. Through a mix of brute force and magical artistry, the feat was accomplished, and the Giants' Dance was reassembled upon Salisbury Plain.

So runs the earliest account of the foundation of Stonehenge in Geoffrey of Monmouth's twelfth-century epic *History of the Kings of Britain*, and, for many years, it was the dominant theory as to the great monument's origin

"Although strongly associated with the summer solstice today, it is likely that Stonehenge was a place of winter, a shrine to the ancestors that was at its peak in the coldest season"

and purpose.[1] As other explanations developed, involving everyone from the Druids to the Ancient Greeks, it seemed unlikely that Merlin would get a second hearing. If Stonehenge is anything, however, it is open to interpretation, and some 900 years after Geoffrey's description, scholars have once again turned west for the site's origin story. In an echo of the Merlin legend, the visionary archaeologist Mike Parker Pearson proposed that the bluestones of Stonehenge (sourced from the Preseli Hills of Pembrokeshire, Wales) were first erected as a local stone circle before being disassembled and transported to Wiltshire. Part of the A303's favourite Neolithic temple was second-hand, pre-loved by earlier worshippers. The proposed site for this proto-Stonehenge is Waun Mawn, the remains of an unfinished circle in the Preseli Hills, not far from where the bluestones were quarried. Although recent excavations have shown that the monument couldn't have held all of Stonehenge's bluestones, there are similarities with the Wiltshire super-complex: the diameter of Waun Mawn was 110m (120yd), exactly the same as Stonehenge's enclosing ditch, and it is also aligned to the solstice.[2]

Debate will continue over Parker Pearson's disassembling theory, but it is a powerful and poetic idea with a clear message for the present. For unlike Merlin's triumph over the Irish, the dismantling and re-erection of the stone

Sunshine on sarsens in the winter of 2018

circle can be seen as a unifying act: Neolithic migrants from Wales took down their cherished stone circle and delivered it to an already holy landscape. Imagine the cooperation this would have taken; imagine how special these particular stones must have been. As the archaeologist writes, "Bluestones were brought to the land of sarsen stones and installed at a sacred *axis mundi*, where the sky and the earth were envisioned in cosmic harmony, and where people of different cultural and regional origins might gather for collective monument-building and feasting."[3]

Today, Waun Mawn is an evocative and spectral remnant of a stone circle. When you climb up from the road below, the site's lone standing stone reveals itself first, while other megaliths lie recumbent in the vicinity. It is a desolate yet beguiling location, the Preseli Hills providing a majestic moorland amphitheatre for whatever rites were once observed here. And Stonehenge's clock can be wound further back in the Preselis. The quarries identified as the source of the bluestones lie near Waun Mawn, and one of these, the particularly fascinating outcrop of Craig Rhos-y-felin, is only a short walk from Pentre Ifan, providing the opportunity for a killer double-site hit: a powerful dolmen and the Stonehenge quarry barely three kilometres apart.

Situated alongside the watery babble of the Afon Brynberian, Craig Rhos-y-felin's jagged angles are patterned with yellow gorse even in winter. It looks, somewhat surprisingly, exactly how you would imagine a megalithic quarry: blocks lie seemingly ready for transport, while the outcrop itself appears to bear the mark of incisions used to prise away great chunks of stone. The slabs that lie at the foot of the tor seem to call out, not yet fully born, pleading to be employed in a sacred alignment. The quarry is a place to stand and wonder what it was about these hills, this rock, that had such an impact upon ancient people. Winter is, perhaps, the perfect time for such contemplation.

Although strongly associated with the summer solstice today, it is likely that Stonehenge was a place of winter, a shrine to the ancestors that was at its peak in the coldest season, the period when death is most vividly drawn. The nearby Durrington Walls complex was the site of a midwinter feast that could have brought people from as far away as Scotland. Analysis of animal remains has shown that folk descended on the area from across Britain at this time. Mike Parker Pearson and his colleague Ramilisonina have suggested that the monument builders used timber to symbolise the living and stone the dead.

As Durrington featured a timber circle aligned on the midwinter sunrise, the raves that took place there were preparations for the work that lay ahead – the veneration of the ancestors by the construction of and ritual observance at Stonehenge. When we see Stonehenge as a spirit place, it makes sense that Neolithic migrants would have spent so much effort transporting their sacred bluestones from the Preseli Hills to this new land, to Britain's *axis mundi*. They wanted their ancestors here too.

For the modern visitor to Wiltshire's sacred hub, there is much to navigate before approaching these ancestors. Stonehenge is, as you would expect, afforded the facilities befitting a tourist attraction of worldwide renown. The visitor centre provides an immersive wraparound video of the site through the ages, alongside a wealth of prehistoric artefacts, and there is, of course, the inevitable gift shop. Locating the centre away from the monument has proven useful, however, not least because it pushes people to engage with the wider Stonehenge landscape and its associated monuments. It is a wonderful thing to walk towards the stones through the woods in winter, leaving the modern world behind as you approach the Greater Cursus and its barrows. The true power of the site is still felt in this season, and especially at the winter solstice.

As well as the feats of prehistoric engineering, the timescales involved at Stonehenge are mind boggling. Around 8000 BCE, three large pine posts were already standing proud on the site, their purpose unknown; were these totems linked to the monument that would be built thousands of years later? Perhaps the area's significance was already known to Mesolithic people due to the presence of what are termed "periglacial stripes" – natural ridge lines in the landscape uncovered by archaeologists.[4] The periglacial stripes in the vicinity of Stonehenge just happen to align with the midwinter solstice. For ancient people, the ground around here was literally pointing to the unification of heaven and earth.

A ditch with internal and external banks was constructed at Stonehenge around 3000 BCE, and building in stone accelerated some five hundred years later, with the raising of the mighty trilithons and the lintel-topped sarsen circle. One of the joys of a winter solstice visit is the opportunity to get inside the inner circle, where the energy of the site really intensifies and the work of the ancient builders can truly be appreciated. Here, the enormous sarsen trilithons tower above you, their remarkable construction the source

"Part of the A303's favourite Neolithic temple was second-hand, pre-loved by earlier worshippers"

Bluestone source: the ancient quarry at Craig Rhos-y-felin

of endless speculation. These slabs had a much shorter journey than the bluestones, with most being sourced from West Woods near Marlborough. A vibe-laden location full of hidden history, West Woods has evidence of activity from the Mesolithic onwards and is scattered with sarsens. Many of these were broken up in the Victorian period, but several behemoths can still be seen among the trees. Gigantic stones, some weighing in at over thirty

tonnes, were carefully chosen and dragged with Herculean effort to their current home through the magnificent landscape of the Vale of Pewsey.

A visit to Waun Mawn, Craig Rhos-y-felin or West Woods allows us to hear an echo of Stonehenge its infancy, and to connect with its potential as a place for unification. We like to imagine that the Merlin myth carries the faint charge of memory – of stones from the west brought to the most sacred spot of them all, where people from across Britain could come together. Through feasting, building and remembering those who had passed over, disparate communities bonded for a midwinter festival, resolved differences and looked ahead to warmer days. This spirit of unification, of celebration in a storied landscape, feels well overdue for a wider revival.

WALKING NOTES

You don't need us to tell you how to get to Stonehenge, but there is plenty to explore in the wider landscape in addition to the legendary monument itself. Woodhenge is found at SU 15074 43380 and Durrington Walls is next door at SU 14809 43634. Tucked away nearby is the enigmatic Cuckoo Stone (SU 14658 43345), which ley hunter Alfred Watkins noted was aligned with the Greater Cursus. Adjacent to the Cursus (which predates the first phase of Stonehenge) are many Bronze Age round barrows (SU 11854 42742), showing that this landscape remained important for a remarkably long period of time.

At Waun Mawn, there is a group of stones at SN 08369 34039 and a solitary menhir at SN 08026 33946. There is no dedicated parking, but there is the odd spot to park up along the B4329. Begin walking up the hill at a fork in the road at SN 08366 33651. You can then follow the track and head across the moorland to the stones. Map and compass are recommended for tracking down these megaliths. Craig Rhos-y-felin is around 5km (3.1 miles) from Waun Mawn (SN 11668 36166). We walked from Pentre Ifan (see walking notes on page 43). Avoid accessing Craig Rhos-y-felin from the east – the twisting road and deep ford make for a tricky route.

West Woods has a car park at SU 16226 66659. From here you can explore the woods. A standing stone can be tracked down in Broom Copse (SU 16244 65284) – a proper prehistoric Easter egg. A long barrow is found at SU 15684 65629, just off the path that skirts the southern section of the woodland. Sarsens that didn't make the Stonehenge cut are scattered through the trees.

Stonehenge supremo, Mike Parker Pearson

LUD'S CHURCH

Arthurian myth spills from a remarkable fissure

STAFFORDSHIRE, ENGLAND (SJ 98704 65667)
OS EXPLORER OL24

Sir Gawain and the Green Knight pulses through the British imagination. The epic Arthurian poem survives in a single fourteenth-century manuscript and remained unpublished for some 450 years, and yet, since its rediscovery, it has been told and retold again and again. From Tolkien's faithful translation of the dialect verse to the psychedelic medievalism of David Lowery's film *The Green Knight*, the narrative's combination of fatalistic quest and enigmatic symbolism continues to work its subtle magic.

The tale's initial setting is a wintry one: it begins at the court of King Arthur on New Year's Eve. A gigantic figure of pure green, bearing an axe and a holly bough and riding a green horse, interrupts the festivities and challenges any knight to strike him with his axe, providing he may return the blow in one year and one day's time. It is Sir Gawain who takes up the task, decapitating the Green Knight with a single stroke. However, rather than falling dead, the uninvited guest picks up his head by the hair and mounts his green horse, "the grim corpse bleeding freely the while".[1]

It is then Sir Gawain's quest to find the Green Knight and the destiny that awaits him. The stranger has told him of his house:

241

"Many men know me as the knight of the Green Chapel, and if thou askest, thou shalt not fail to find me."[2] The Green Chapel is the end point of this story and a site of deep mystery. It is a place of green even in the depths of winter, a place where death and rebirth collide.

Approaching the chasm known as Lud's Church on a winter's morning, it is easy to see why, in the 1950s, runologist and professor of English R. W. V. Elliott could confidently suggest this spot as the Green Knight's abode. The Gawain poet has long been thought a native of North Staffordshire or South Cheshire, an inference drawn from his description of scenery and use of dialect, and here, in the Dark Peak, on the very edge of Staffordshire, the terrain certainly feels right.

Lud's Church lies in the woodland of Back Forest, above the tumbling chatter of the River Dane. This is a landscape of jutting outcrops and erratic, moss-covered boulders that look, at first glance, like ruined Cyclopean structures looming out from the trees. As you climb, the sound of the river gives way to the uncanny quiet of the wood.

Once through the entrance to Lud's Church, the temperature shifts down when you ascend and then descend an approximation of steps. The walls of Millstone Grit that tower above are blanketed with lichens, ferns and sprouting sprigs of holly, while precarious trees dangle from the summit. When alone, sounds in the fissure come to the fore: the dripping of water, the shuffle of your footsteps on the rock, all slightly treated by the resonance of this unusual natural architecture. The viridescent sheer walls, cut-throughs and hollows, formed by an enormous landslip sometime after the last ice age, cast a strangely magnetic spell. But to Sir Gawain, the site was eerie and unholy, rather than inspiring. Of course, the knight knew that the keeper of this chasm was close at hand.

What can we say about the Green Knight, this most intriguing character of Arthurian legend? His pagan tones ring out clearly: he is as verdant as the Green Man of folklore, with his holly

bough and beard like a bush. But, perhaps, he is also written to show us that the natural world, the wild, unchanging roots of the world, should not be underestimated or forgotten.

The Gawain poet goes to great lengths to describe human achievements – shining armour, delicate silks and mighty castles – and yet, all will be useless when the Green Knight's axe falls. He is the tester of knights, and also their judge. If we trust honestly in him, and hold nature in balance with mankind, perhaps we ourselves can be renewed, re-enchanted. When the Knight allows Sir Gawain to sustain what the poet Simon Armitage describes as a blow "just skimming the skin and finely snicking the fat of

"It is a place of green even in the depths of winter, a place where death and rebirth collide"

the flesh", Gawain is effectively reborn, saved from a seemingly inevitable fate.[3] Arthur's knight lives again, but his future is forever altered.

In Alan Garner's novel *Boneland*, Lud's Church also appears as a liminal place where changes are wrought. "Ludcruck" is a sacred cleft of death and remembrance for the Watcher, the Mesolithic shaman we follow in the novel. He works funerary rites and ritual art in the depths, with the hopes that winter will fade and beasts will be plentiful across the land. Marking the death of the old year and encouraging the coming of new life is as ancient a practice as can be imagined, and Garner's prehistoric character is brilliantly rendered, his concerns shown to be timeless.

Garner knows this land and its lore, and his choice of Lud's Church as a key location is a meaningful one. When he came to read *Sir Gawain and the Green Knight* in its original form, the writer was surprised that there were so many footnotes to clarify the poem's regional Middle English: "I didn't need many of them, nor did my father (who had left school at fifteen), if I read certain pieces to him in our shared modern Cheshire dialect."[4] The Gawain poet's language is the language of Garner's family and his ancestors, who have lived in the Cheshire village of Alderley Edge for hundreds of years. The writer cites *Sir Gawain* as a major influence on his work, "an English treasure", and, perhaps, *Boneland* subtly hints at the epic poem throughout: an axe, a hood of green, an opening injection that leaves "just a scratch". Clues or coincidences? Garner's meticulous nature as a writer suggests the former.

Boneland also demonstrates a fascination with a plastic and porous notion of time itself. It is a take that appears in many of Garner's novels: events can form a resonating loop, so that the present coexists with the past. Colin, the polymath we track in alternation with the Watcher, is the child character first introduced fifty years earlier in *The Weirdstone of Brisingamen*. With no memory of his childhood, he searches the stars at Jodrell Bank Observatory, in a scientific mirror of the ancient shaman's ritual actions in the chasm. Time is layered and looped, but sometimes we can peer between the cracks. And here in Ludcruck, this mythic chapel of perpetual green, perhaps we can get more than a glimpse of what has gone before and what is yet to come.

WALKING NOTES
You can park for Lud's Church at a small car park at SJ 99902 66212, and then walk following the river and up into Back Forest. The chasm itself is found at SJ 98704 65667. A rambling soundtrack could be provided by Nocturnal Emissions' darkly luminous 1989 LP, *Stoneface*, which includes tracks titled for Lud's Church, the Grey Ladies stone circle and other Peak District landmarks. The album's ominous drones and clattering

organic percussion can provide some much-needed propulsion on the climb above the River Dane.

There is much speculation on the etymology of Lud's Church. A group of proto-Protestant church reformers called Lollards may have met here in the fifteenth century, with one of their number being a Walter de Ludank. The group would meet in secret due to their then-heretical beliefs and, according to legend, de Ludank was captured in an ambush here which also killed his granddaughter. An effigy of this "Lady Lud" stood on the site for many years. It was, in fact, and no less strangely, a ship's figurehead linked to a local landowner. Other theories include the identification of Lud's Church with the Irish god Lugh, and this area as a place of offering and sacrifice.

BURGHEAD

A night of fire ushers in the (Old) New Year

MORAY, SCOTLAND [NJ 10919 69184]
OS EXPLORER 423

A unique identity is preserved in the small coastal town of Burghead in Moray. Built on an isolated peninsula that juts out into the cold, crystalline waters of the Moray Firth, it is an unpretentious wonder, a place that is perfect for wandering and exploration. Burghead once belonged to a very real King in the North: it was a major hub for the Picts, a people whose enigmatic legacy still hums in this part of Scotland and is threaded through Burghead today.

Even in the winter chill, the walking is good here. A trail runs across Moray's coastline of savage cliffs and sandy beaches while, just outside of Burghead, the woodland of Roseisle Forest is perfect strolling territory. Within Burghead itself, however, there is one killer draw in wintertime. On 11 January, a burning barrel is walked around the darkened town before being ceremonially torched in a mighty, precarious blaze on top of a hill within the old Pictish fort. The burning of the Clavie is a ritual that has somehow survived down the centuries as a unique Brocher (as Burghead natives call themselves) custom.

If you walk along Burghead's seafront, on the Moray Coast Trail, the Firth is choppy and the dolphins that happily frolic in the summer months are nowhere to be seen. The small harbour is dotted with bright,

247

well-maintained working boats, while a couple of older wooden vessels lean sadly in empty plots. Past the harbour, the sandstone cliffs rear up. A set of steps is hewn into the rock, a rusting chain keeping you on track as you ascend towards the remains of the Pictish fort, initially constructed in the fourth century. As with everything in Burghead, there is an unfussy presentation attached to this incredibly significant archaeological site. This is a living, working community and the fort's squat, white visitor centre is nestled next to houses and gardens on the promontory.

"The closer you get to the blackness, the further the temperature drops"

Finds began turning up at Burghead in the nineteenth century when the new town was being built. Remarkable images of bulls, incised on stone slabs and thought to represent fertility and strength, were pulled from the ground. The stones can be found in replica inside the visitor centre, and their enchanting presence is only one of many Pictish expressions of art in stone. The rich archaeology began to put Burghead on the map of venerable Scottish sites, but Brochers will tell you they always knew their home was a site of great power. Such knowledge meant it was no surprise when an ancient well was discovered in Burghead's newly developing streets as workers searched for a water source. Local tradition had always told of a hidden well.

Today, you can request the key to the well at the visitor centre and, with a few simple directions, you are off towards the town proper, entering its distinctive grid pattern of streets. Beyond the padlocked door, neatly set in a wall between residences, you are confronted by steps that descend to an inky portal. The closer you get to the blackness, the further the temperature drops. Even on warm days, your breath mists as you stand on the greenish steps that are eventually topped by an archway. The well itself is fed by an underground spring and encased in a beautifully worked chamber that features a pedestal, sink and walkway around the edge of the pool. It is an uncanny place, with unusual acoustics able to amplify and reverberate voices in the strangest ways.

Speculation has, of course, raged about its purpose. The Picts were known to have form in drowning as a mode of execution,[1] and so some have been tempted to interpret the space as a ritual drowning pool. Although, as one Brocher insisted to us, "If you're going to drown someone, there's a lot of sea over there!" Indeed, perhaps such an interpretation plays into the hands of those who would paint the Picts as barbarians (the very word coming from an association with painted skin in battle). Another suggestion is the well was used as part of a cult devoted to a water divinity, a notion supported by the discovery here of a sculpted human head. Despite the ominous approach, the vibe of the well today is certainly one of peaceful contemplation, as echoing water drips into the pool buried deep into the earth of this peninsula.

With the well's door firmly locked, the walk back to the visitor centre to return the key takes you past the Doorie Hill, the hump on which each Old New Year is welcomed in by the Clavie Crew and their pyrotechnics. The blackened plinth that holds the burning barrel and its raging incendiaries is surprisingly close to the neighbours' back gardens, but the weird juxtaposition of everyday and ritualised, numinous spaces is a key aspect of Burghead's appeal. The Clavie has been burned here for as long as anyone can remember and, certainly, much longer than that. With the reform of the calendar in the eighteenth century to move to the Gregorian system, eleven days were famously lost, but Brochers simply decided to double up the celebrations – keeping 1 January and 11 January as festive occasions, with the Clavie being burned on the latter. Nowadays, the ritual can attract thousands of visitors, with the elected Clavie King in charge of proceedings and accompanied by his Clavie Crew. (Only those born a Brocher are eligible to be a member.) Smouldering remnants of the Clavie are prized as good luck charms, and it is not uncommon for Brochers in distant lands to request a piece be saved for them.

249

Burghead is a curious place, where contemporary concerns rub shoulders with relics of an ancient culture and traditions that stretch back into the mists of time. In winter, the coming of the Brochers' New Year is still celebrated with marvellous, idiosyncratic gusto. Witnessing the Burning of the Clavie connects us to a deep sense of community, and affords us a glimpse of how the Picts themselves may have marked the year's death and rebirth.

WALKING NOTES

There are several car parks and plentiful roadside parking in Burghead. Parking at Burghead Beach (by the caravan park at NJ 11385 68636) allows you to explore the settlement and then track back for a stroll into Roseisle Forest if you wish. The fort and its small but excellent visitor centre can be found at NJ 10919 69184. You can borrow the key to the well at the visitor centre. Plan ahead if you are visiting for the Burning of the Clavie, as parking will be trickier.

Burnt offerings: the Burning of the Clavie in 1975

CHEPSTOW

English and Welsh traditions entwine in a liminal border town

MONMOUTHSHIRE, WALES [ST 53411 94138]
OS EXPLORER 167

The Mari Lwyd is the most enigmatic of Welsh folkloric figures. A beribboned horse's skull with shining eyes, the beast is carried on a pole by her bearer, who hides beneath a white cloth. The character was once a popular guest at Christmas and New Year's festivities, but her customs waned in the nineteenth century before undergoing a spirited revival over the last forty years or so. It is in the cold of a Chepstow January that one of the most fascinating appearances of the Mari Lwyd takes place, combining English and Welsh traditions in a town right on the border.

Chepstow sits on the Welsh banks of the River Wye, where Monmouthshire meets Gloucestershire. It is the definition of a liminal place, a brackish borderland dominated by its imposing castle, constructed shortly after the Norman Conquest. This was the first of many stone fortifications built in what became known as the Welsh Marches (meaning frontier in this sense) to show the strength of the new Norman lords and guard against Welsh raids. However, long before the conquerors laid the foundations of Chepstow Castle, Offa, the Anglo-Saxon king of Mercia, had built his famous dyke in the area, separating his lands from the Welsh kingdom of Powys. Today, the beautiful 285km trail, the Offa's Dyke Path, begins (or ends) at Sedbury Cliffs, a mile to

253

the east of Chepstow. On a cold winter's day, Chepstow itself remains an inspiring place for a wander.

The castle is, of course, the main draw, and rightly so. Aptly, for a place with such a deep relationship with boundaries, Chepstow Castle's remarkable oak doors are particularly significant, being the oldest in Europe. Having been dated to 1190, they are now safely displayed inside the castle, although they don't exactly look fragile: never actually breached, even Cromwell's army chose to demolish a wall rather than attack via the gates during the English Civil War.

The castle, situated high above the Wye on its natural clifftop promontory, has inspired artists and poets for centuries, not least

"In her vigorous movements, bare skull and shroud-like attire, the Mari Lwyd speaks of both life and death"

Brazilian metal legends Sepultura, who recorded the ecstatic, percussive "Kaiowas" from 1993's *Chaos A.D.* at the site. The track is doubtless enhanced by the ancient acoustic properties of the castle; photographs of the session show the thrashers recording against a backdrop of Norman stonework, while Chepstow's gulls can be heard calling over the count-in.

If Chepstow has charmed metal pioneers, it has also become an important destination for lovers of British folklore and custom. For several years, the town's liminality has been a central part of the Chepstow Wassail Mari Lwyd celebration, which usually takes place (barring pandemic interruption) each January. Although established fairly recently, the tradition combines venerable elements, including the wassailing custom and the parading of the Mari Lwyd. At a key point, the English and Welsh revellers meet on the border at the Old Wye Bridge to exchange flags.

The word "wassail" is derived from the Old English *wæs þu hæl,* meaning "be in good health". The greeting would be met with *drinc hæl*, meaning "drink and be healthy". Wassails themselves are generally divided into two categories: the house-visiting and orchard-visiting customs, and both traditions are associated with winter festivities, such as Christmas and Twelfth Night celebrations.

House-visiting wassails may have begun in the Middle Ages, when farmworkers would approach the home of the local lord to receive gifts and hospitality in return for blessings. A boozy good-luck drink was offered to the household (often spiced ale or cider from a bowl) and songs were sung. The wassails found in their revived form across the country today are mostly variations of the orchard-visiting custom. Often associated with English cider-producing counties, wassailers sing songs beneath the apple trees, offer cider to their roots, and bang pots and pans to scare away evil spirits and wake the trees for the year ahead. But at Chepstow it's party poppers that provide the rumpus, while a decorated apple tree is pulled towards the Old Wye Bridge on a cart for the purposes of the festivities. Good luck and a fine harvest are the wassailers' aims, and the custom is one of those rare examples of a direct link to the pagan past.[1] Communities have always gathered to look ahead with hope as the days slowly lengthen.

The combination of this ancient custom with the Welsh tradition of the Mari Lwyd lends the Chepstow festival its particular flavour. Once the English have been met on the bridge, they are invited across the river for the Mari Lwyd ceremony at Chepstow Museum. It is here that the Mari knocks on the door to be let in. Originally the beast would engage in a contest of singing and riddling before she was finally allowed over the threshold with her party, to partake in the grub and grog within.[2]

In her vigorous movements, bare skull and shroud-like attire, the Mari Lwyd speaks of both life and death. This duality was captured perfectly by the poet Vernon Watkins, whose *Ballad of the Mari Lwyd* also considers the nature of New Year's Eve, the calendrical cusp when the Mari would often appear. The uncertain flickering between life and death, light and dark, is evident throughout the poem.

On a winter's evening, in this boundary place of ancient portals, it is easy to see the presence of the Mari Lwyd and the wassail custom as a connection with a bygone age, a link between the living and the dead. However, it is more than a tradition alone; in its creativity and unifying spirit, it is also a defiantly hopeful celebration, a pointer to the year ahead.

WALKING NOTES

At the time of writing, the Chepstow Wassail Mari Lwyd is on hiatus. However, there are many wassails held in winter, with notable examples in Stroud, Much Marcle (at Weston's Cider), Streatham Common, Sandford (Thatchers Cider) and Yarlington. The Mari Lwyd can still be found in Caerleon, Dinas Mawddwy and Llangynwyd, the latter village hosting a particularly old iteration of the tradition.

SILBURY HILL

An enormous sacred mound rises from deep time

```
WILTSHIRE, ENGLAND (SU 10008 68530)
OS EXPLORER 157
```

How do you wrap your head around Silbury Hill? This earthen mound, the largest in Europe of prehistoric origin, has haunted so many throughout the ages, produced so many theories, that even getting a grip on the commentary surrounding the structure is a daunting task. In the twenty-first century, Silbury remains a titanic disturbance – a colossal echo of community collaboration that has as much to say about our future as our past.

Silbury Hill sits within a vast ritual landscape, with the super-henge of Avebury, its stones and emanating avenues, at its heart, and other key sites – the Sanctuary, West Kennet Long Barrow and Beckhampton Cove – spread across the wider area. Erected below Waden Hill, Silbury was probably one of the last, and most important, monuments to be completed within this sacred wonderland.

Even in winter, Silbury is at one with Wiltshire's flora and fauna, not dominating its natural surroundings but emerging from them. As noted by William Stukeley, one of the first to recognise the enormous importance of the Avebury landscape, the way that the monument builders harmonised with nature is remarkable: "They have made plains and hills, valleys, springs and rivers contribute to form a temple of three miles in length. They have stamp'd a whole country with the impress of this sacred character."[1] For the writer

259

"In the twenty-first century, Silbury remains a titanic disturbance — a colossal echo of community collaboration that has as much to say about our future as our past"

Michael Dames, Silbury Hill was central to a Neolithic goddess religion – it was the pregnant belly ("the harvest womb") of the Great Mother Goddess, surrounded by a moat representing her body. Here, the mound *is* the natural world – fertility incarnate.[2]

Approaching the mound from Avebury village, following the route of the River Kennet, its form never fails to enchant. Silbury is visually elusive; it seems to appear subtly different on each visit, and especially when viewed from different angles. Such peculiar qualities have transfixed the artist David Inshaw, who has repeatedly painted the site in all its numerous weathers and seasons. Inshaw's image of Silbury in the snow shows shadow creeping across a perfectly white mound. Millennia ago, however, the hill would have glistened white all year round, an immense sacred beacon of bright, smoothed chalk.

With so much invested in Silbury, its site was no doubt carefully chosen. For the ley line enthusiasts of the 1970s, Silbury sat on a significant ley that took in Bincknoll Castle and Marden Henge, as well as Avebury itself.[3] The visionary John Michell went further, seeing Silbury as being located on a line of "dragon force", an energy with parallels in ancient Chinese geomancy that was once tapped into to ensure the land's fertility. Although links to dragon energy will always prove tricky to ascertain, anyone who has visited Silbury in all weathers will know that it is connected to water, almost appearing as an island among

The sarsen stone façade at West Kennet Long Barrow

Desire lines: a view of Silbury Hill en route from Swallowhead Spring

marshy fields on occasions. Perhaps the reason for the mound's location lies to the south of Silbury Hill, in the form of Swallowhead Spring.

Today, Swallowhead Spring lies across the busy Bath Road from Silbury, tucked away at the far right of a farmer's field. It feels off the beaten track – the springs reject signposting, and the aforementioned field is populated by cattle and borders on a swamp in some months. However, it's easy to see why Swallowhead has felt special for so long. Even some of the cheesier hippie detritus that accumulates here can't detract from the child-like pleasure of walking over the massive sarsen stepping stones to see the sacred waters rising from the earth. It may have been this strange, quiet place, a source of the River Kennet, which held a particular value for Neolithic people, and led them to begin the construction of the enormous mound. The location of Silbury's shadowy sister site upstream (known as Merlin's Mount and found within the grounds of Marlborough College) suggests that the life-giving properties of water featured strongly in the mound builders' thinking.

A short walk from Swallowhead, above the gentle flow of the Kennet, sits another potent site in this landscape. West Kennet Long Barrow is a masterpiece of Neolithic engineering, a building project commenced around 3650 BCE. Like Wayland's Smithy (see page 148), it features an impressive façade of sarsen stones. This long barrow can be explored more deeply than Wayland's Smithy, however. Its five chambers are wonderfully constructed, with four off the 12m (39ft) passageway and one large chamber at the end. The roof is also much higher than at some other long barrows, such as Belas Knap or Stoney Littleton, meaning you don't have to duck and are less likely to smash your head (something we have repeatedly done in chambered tombs). It's a calm, reflective spot, and you can see why it's so popular with New Age adherents. The view from the long barrow is wondrous too, taking in Silbury, Windmill Hill and the shape of East Kennet Barrow – West Kennet's enormous, unexcavated twin. This is a landscape developed over millennia; West Kennet would already have been ancient when the chalk was being piled up on Silbury below.

It's possible, of course, to walk further out, past the mysterious Sanctuary with its concrete marker blocks, and onto the ancient Ridgeway track. From here, you can yomp along the chalk path until you take a right into the beautiful expanse of Fyfield Down, its endless sarsen stones and weathered thorn trees lending the place a special character all of its own, especially in the low winter

"The visionary John Michell went further, seeing Silbury as being located on a line of "dragon force", an energy with parallels in ancient Chinese geomancy that was once tapped into to ensure the land's fertility"

sun. Keep walking and you will soon spy the mighty dolmen of Devil's Den (see front cover), one of the most magical locations in these isles, and relatively unbothered by visitors. If ever there was a place for re-enchantment, the Devil's Den is it. Local folklore holds that Satan arrives each night with eight white oxen and attempts to pull off the monument's capstone. He is aided in his endeavours by a white rabbit with burning eyes, but the fiend's efforts are always in vain. There is power in the stones.

Walking back towards the massive earthen mound visited earlier, it is hard not to marvel once more at the timescales involved in this sacred topography. A hazel twig excavated from the heart of Silbury Hill has been dated to around 4,500 years ago and recent work, spurred on by a partial collapse of the earthwork in the year 2000, suggests that the monument took hundreds of years to reach its final form.[4] The mound, along with many other ancient structures, is testament to a remarkable feat of social enterprise by a people who took a long-term view of their culture – an attempt, over many years, to leave a lasting mark imbued with great meaning. This is also suggestive of the cohesive work of a society, rather than the orders of one mighty chief. With 248,000 cubic metres of material used in the mound's construction, archaeologists such

263

as Alasdair Whittle point to a culture devoted to a ritual cycle to explain the heroic investment of time and muscle required. This sacred cycle could have been driven by "myths of return, and belief in renewal, allied to a desire to both honour and emulate the ancestors, in a matrix of cyclical, ritual time".[5]

Perhaps in this reading of Silbury we can find lessons for our current society. The chronic short-termism of the twenty-first century renders any endeavour outlasting a single human lifetime unthinkable, a place where long-view projects – from the Svalbard Global Seed Vault to the Clock of the Long Now – are seen as curious footnotes rather than society's core focus. By connecting with ancient sites that required enormous amounts of collaboration and concentration over generations, we approach an altered mindset, and allow ourselves to ask what we will leave for our ancestors to continue. This point also resonates with a prescient note in John Michell's thinking, for if we are to work over extended time periods we must, necessarily, care for the land upon which the work takes place. Michell encourages us to think of Earth, "not as an expendable launching-pad for adventures among alien planets, but as our most precious inheritance, our promised and potential natural paradise".[6]

WALKING NOTES

Parking for Silbury Hill can be found at su 09665 68592. However, it is great to stroll out from Avebury itself and see the mound emerge. A path begins opposite the National Trust car park (su 09937 69541) and allows you to follow the route of the River Kennet towards Silbury Hill. You can get closer to the mound by turning right at su 10138 68879, or carry on along the river, before crossing the road at su 10395 68383. As mentioned, the springs can be found at the bottom of a field (su 10112 68079). The area gets very marshy, so waterproof boots are best, especially in winter. Rejoin the path and cross the bridge at su 10425 68192. Then you can head up to West Kennet Long Barrow (su 10509 67743), enjoying the views of the World Heritage Site.

From West Kennet Long Barrow, you can walk to the Sanctuary and the start of the Ridgeway path (su 11877 68079). There is some parking here. After heading up the Ridgeway, you can take a right towards Fyfield Down at su 12499 70837, crossing the horse gallops carefully. The Devil's Den can be found at su 15208 69652. Bulls are sometimes kept in the area, so you may prefer to access the dolmen from the Bath Road at su 15646 68845.

TRELLECH

A pocket-sized acreage densely packed with enchantment

MONMOUTHSHIRE, WALES (SO 50042 05483)
OS EXPLORER OL14

T rellech is, in some respects, an uncertain place. The village's very name is contested – you'll encounter signs for Tryleg, Trelleck, Trellech and Trelech depending on the angle of your approach. This hazy, atypical feel extends to the monuments here, the importance of which seems to exceed the current size of the community. Indeed, rumours of a forgotten medieval town beneath Trellech have been borne out by recent excavations, visible alongside the archaeologists' Portaloos in a nearby field. More discoveries no doubt await. There is, however, one thing that Trellech is very definite about: a deep affection for its ancient sites and intersecting layers of lore.

Trellech's Rosetta Stone lies inside the Church of St Nicholas. Here, the sculpted side panels of a seventeenth-century sundial bear witness to the village's mysteries: its mound, its stones and its Virtuous Well. Once standing proud in the village centre, the sundial was eventually moved indoors to protect it from the elements. Observing the venerable, chiselled image of three pagan standing stones within this medieval church is a remarkable thing, and it is certainly worth pretending you can read Latin and donning the attitude of a Jamesian academic as you decipher the inscription, mumbling, "MAIOR SAXIS – greater in its stones; MAXIMA FONTE – greatest in its well", as though unravelling some ancient riddle.

The mound commemorated on the sundial is known as Tump Terret. Its associated inscription laments "Oh! How many are buried here!" – a reference to the legend that the mound is the resting place of those slain in a conflict between the last crowned Anglo-Saxon English king, Harold Godwinson, and the Welsh. The site has now been identified as the remnants of a small Norman castle which belonged to the De Clare family. Like all of Trellech's key monuments, the Tump is accompanied by three stages of parish pride – a green gate commemorating the Festival of Britain in 1951, a weathered steel information panel (Trellech School History Trail, 1986) and a more recent board detailing the history and lore of the site, compiled by local children and their teachers. In Trellech, the ancient and the magical are woven into the identity of the village and celebrated unpretentiously. They're a given.

Tump Terret itself emerges ziggurat-like, past swanky barn conversions and their attendant SUVs. This is the remaining motte of the motte and bailey castle, and today its sides ripple with possible paths to the summit, an undulating inverted bowl of green. A summer house was once built on the top of the mound, with flagrant disregard for the supposed curse that befalls those who disturb it. The view over the surrounding landscape perhaps warranted tempting fate.

Not far from Tump Terret, and accessed by tracking the route of a babbling stream across a sheep field, lie the three megaliths of Harold's Stones, a monument that definitely deserves to be more widely known. The stones have a similar feel to Avebury's menhirs, whose ancient sacred alignments are juxtaposed with layers of subsequent history within the bounds of an idyllic village. Unlike Avebury's stones, however, these three are composed of a conglomerate rock called pudding stone, which holds vivid quartz pebbles and lends the megaliths an almost Brutalist concrete quality. They are arranged in a row, apparently in size order, with even the smallest reaching well over two metres (6.6ft). Approached from the standard-issue Trellech Festival of Britain gate, the stones appear straight, but get side on and they reveal wild leans, with the largest presenting particularly suggestively.

Sunrise is the perfect time to visit Harold's Stones, especially in winter. The early bird is rewarded with a slow reveal of colour, as the stones morph from deep blacks to a complex collection of hues drawn from lichen, shadowed grooves and the unusual conglomerate rock itself. It's a site of great energy, but proceed with caution if you get your dowsing rods out. Druid Laurence Main reports that the uprights have been known to repel dowsers, providing tingling

"In one tale, they are said to have arrived in the village when flung from the Black Mountains by the wizard Jack o' Kent during one of his regular chucking competitions with the Devil"

sensations and intense push back.[1] The megalithic energy signal emitted from these antenna especially strong, it seems.

The folklore, as ever, has had its say on the stones. In one tale, they are said to have arrived in the village when flung from the Black Mountains by the wizard Jack o' Kent during one of his regular chucking competitions with the Devil, although their current name derives from the idea that they mark the site of the defeat of three Welsh elders by King Harold. Their true origins lie much earlier, in the Bronze Age, but perhaps talk of Harold preserves a folk memory of the stones' use as an assembly point for those fighting the English king, or even as a site of conflict with the invaders from beyond Offa's Dyke.

However, Trellech's most important venue may be the well that is found a short walk from Harold's Stones. The sundial's inscription "MAXIMA FONTE" carries some truth: the village is powerfully linked to natural springs and deep wells, and the current Virtuous Well is the last of many ancient springs to be in use here. One local tale states that Harold's Stones lean in order to indicate the position of certain sacred waters in the area. The Virtuous Well is sited next to a stream which flows energetically beneath its footbridge, while nearby trees offer up the colourful tied rags that accompany so many holy springs. Also known as St Anne's Well, it was once a big draw for pilgrims due to its curative qualities, the water said to ease ailments of the eyes in particular.

On stepping down into the sunken stone horseshoe of the well, the great age of the place is apparent. Water seeps across ancient flagstones that lead to an arched recess set within the far wall. Here, a basin collects the water that bubbles from the underworld, while further recesses in the wall provide space for offerings or perhaps cups for those who would have drunk the iron-rich water, the mineral evident in a reddish build-up of sediment between the paving and the wall. Stone benches flank the archway, and would no doubt have supported the aching limbs of weary pilgrims in times gone by as they supped thankfully on the healing water. The Virtuous Well remains a meditative place, a reminder of the network of sacred springs in these parts, not least in nearby Ninewells Wood.

The well is captured beautifully on a striking modern interpretation of Trellech's sundial that currently stands at the village crossroads. Cut from the trunk of a single tree, it incorporates all of the nearby sites of interest. Harold's Stones are carved against a backdrop of flowering hawthorn trees, while a

"In Trellech, the ancient and the magical are woven into the identity of the village and celebrated unpretentiously"

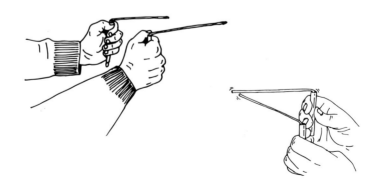

rambler passes through the green gate in the foreground. The sculpture is the latest entry in a long tradition of Trellech acknowledging its sites and stories. This is cherished land. And if history is a wondrous palimpsest on these islands, perhaps it is nowhere more so than in this small Monmouthshire village.

WALKING NOTES

There is a small car park at SO 50087 05282. From here you can take in the key sites. The Church of St Nicholas (and its famous sundial) can be found at SO 50042 05483, and Tump Terret is located at SO 49978 05354. From the Tump, you can follow a signposted path across a sheep field and over the road to Harold's Stones (SO 49929 05144). On your way to the stones, make a stop at the modern interpretation of the sundial described above (SO 50053 05238). The Virtuous Well can be found at SO 50298 05101.

You can soak up the area's connections to sacred waters with a visit to nearby Ninewells Wood, a beautiful Wye Valley woodland (parking 2.5km/1.6 miles from Trellech at SO 51501 03827) once renowned for its healing springs. Spotter's badge if you can find the haunting carving of a fox's face on the stone stile at SO 51403 03482. It is said to have been the creation of a French prisoner held here during the Napoleonic Wars.

AFTERWORD

Over the last year or so we have crisscrossed Britain with cameras and compasses, notepads and Nalgenes, unearthing the seasonal character of this land. Via dusty old tomes and internet deep dives, we teased out nuggets of knowledge and found fresh routes to pursue. Away from the bookshelves and archives, smashed windscreens, sprained ankles and biblical downpours were navigated on our many wanders. And if the pedometers notched up some significant miles, the pubs kept us in (un)healthy balance.

Ultimately, we found that we love this weird, diverse, haunted place even more than we did when we started. The British countryside is a deep resource of rich, transformative strangeness, and one that should be available to us all, regardless of our background or identity. We hope that within these pages there has been something that has sparked a desire in you to step out on the ancient paths that still hum with vibes all across Britain, to savour the traditional spectacles and calendar customs that are woven into our landscape. After all, they belong to everyone. They belong to you.

NOTES

Introduction

1 Paphitis, T. (2020). "Haunted landscapes: place, past and presence", *Time and Mind*, 13:4, pp.341–9.
2 GOV.UK (2021). *Trend Deck 2021: Urbanisation.* [online] GOV.UK. Available at: www.gov.uk/government/publications/trend-deck-2021-urbanisation/trend-deck-2021-urbanisation.
3 Higgs, J. (2017). *Watling Street* [Kindle version]. London: Orion.
4 Fukuyama, F. (1992). *The End of History and the Last Man.* London: Penguin.
5 Fukuyama, F. (1989). "The End of History?", *The National Interest*, 16, pp.3–18. Available at: www.jstor.org/stable/24027184
6 Reynolds, S. (2012). *Retromania: pop culture's addiction to its own past.* London: Faber, pp.x–xi.
7 See Fisher, M. (2014). *Ghosts of My Life: writings on depression, hauntology and lost futures.* Hants: Zero Books.
8 *The Wicker Man Enigma* (2001). Directed by David Gregory [Film].

Cerne Abbas, Dorset

1 University of Gloucestershire (12 May 2021). "National Trust archaeologists surprised by likely age of Cerne Abbas Giant" [online]. Available at: www.glos.ac.uk/content/national-trust-cerne-giant. [Accessed: 15 Dec 2022].
2 Geoffrey, Thompson, A. and Giles, J. A. (1842). *The British History of Geoffrey of Monmouth, in Twelve Books.* London: James Bohn, p.15.

Pentre Ifan, Pembrokeshire

1 Whittle, A. (2004). "Stones that Float to the Sky", in Cummings, V. and Fowler, C. (eds.) *The Neolithic of the Irish Sea: materiality and traditions of practice.* Oxford: Oxbow, pp.81–90.
2 Cummings, V. (2018). "Imagining Prehistoric Landscapes", in Burnham, A. (ed.) *The Old Stones: a field guide to the megalithic sites of Britain and Ireland.* London: Watkins, p.19.
3 See, for example, Tilley, C. (1994). *A Phenomenology of Landscape: places, paths and monuments.* Oxford; Providence: Berg.

The Druids' Temple, North Yorkshire

1 See Headley, G. and Meulenkamp, W. (1999). *Follies, Grottoes & Garden Buildings.* London: Aurum.
2 Williams, L. (2020). *Miracles of Our Own Making: a history of paganism.* London: Reaktion Books, p.155.
3 HL Deb, 26 June 2000, c701.
4 See Rees, G.E. (2020). *Unofficial Britain: journeys through unexpected places.* London: Elliott & Thompson Limited.

Wootton Rivers, Wiltshire

1 Quoted in Simpson, J. and Roud, S. (2000). *A Dictionary of English Folklore.* Oxford; New York: Oxford University Press, p.154.
2 Ibid.
3 See Devereux, P. and Thomson, I. (1979). *The Ley Hunter's Companion: aligned ancient sites: a new study with field guide and maps.* London: Thames and Hudson, pp.134–5.
4 Partridge, J. B. (1915). "Wiltshire Folklore", *Folklore*, 26:2, pp.211–12. DOI: 10.1080/0015587X.1915.9718878

Bix Bottom, Oxfordshire

1 Scovell, A. (2017). *Folk Horror: hours dreadful and things strange.* Leighton Buzzard: Auteur Publishing, p.18.

Tigh nam Bodach, Perth and Kinross

1 Stewart, A. (1986). *Daughters of the Glen.* Aberfeldy: Leura Press, p.17.
2 See Hutton, R. (2022). *Queens of the Wild: pagan goddesses in Christian Europe: an investigation.* New Haven: Yale University Press, p.153.

The Druids' Temple, North Yorkshire (continued)

4 Young, R. (2010). *Electric Eden: unearthing Britain's visionary music.* London: Faber and Faber, p.371.
5 See King, R. (2019). *The Lark Ascending: people, music and landscape in twentieth-century Britain.* London: Faber and Faber.

3 See Ross, A. (2000). *Folklore of the Scottish Highlands* [Kindle version]. Stroud: Tempus.
4 Ibid.

Padstow, Cornwall

1 See Groom, N. (2013). *The Seasons: a celebration of the English year*. London: Atlantic Books, pp.162–3.
2 See Hutton, R. (1996). *The Stations of the Sun: a history of the ritual year in Britain*. Oxford: Oxford University Press.

Cooper's Hill, Gloucestershire

1 See Roud, S. (2008). *The English Year: a month-by-month guide to the nation's customs and festivals, from May Day to Mischief Night*. London: Penguin Books, p.206.

Stanton Drew, Somerset

1 Scurr, R. (2015). *John Aubrey: My Own Life*. New York: New York Review Books, p.155.
2 Simpson, J. and Roud, S. (2000). *A Dictionary of English Folklore*, Oxford: Oxford University Press, p.342.
3 Scurr, R. *John Aubrey*, p.155.
4 Devereux, P. (2001). *Stone Age Soundtracks: the acoustic archaeology of ancient sites*. London: Vega, p.12.

Thaxted, Essex

1 See Cutting, J. (2005). *History and the Morris Dance*. Alton: Dance Books, p.12.
2 Idler. (n.d.). *The Seasonal Festivals of Britain with Ronald Hutton*. [online] Course available at: https://www.idler.co.uk/product/seasonal-festivals-of-britain-with-ronald-hutton/ [Accessed 16 June 2022].

Castlerigg, Cumbria

1 Radcliffe, A. (1796). *A Journey Made in the Summer of 1794, through Holland and the Western Frontier of Germany, with a Return down the Rhine: to which are added observations during a tour to the lakes of Lancashire, Westmoreland, and Cumberland. In two volumes*. London: G. G. and J. Robinson, Paternoster Row, p.446.
2 See Ray, K. and Thomas, J. (2018). *Neolithic Britain: the transformation of social worlds*. Oxford: Oxford University Press, pp.125–6.

Bryn Celli Ddu, Isle of Anglesey

1 www.gutenberg.org. (n.d.). *Ten Days' Tour through the Isle of Anglesea, by John Skinner*. [online] Available at: https://www.gutenberg.org/files/64154/64154-h/64154-h.htm#page44 [Accessed 19 Feb. 2022].
2 Burrow, S. (2010). Bryn Celli Ddu Passage Tomb, Anglesey: Alignment, Construction, Date, and Ritual. *Proceedings of the Prehistoric Society*, 76, pp.249–70.

Avebury, Wiltshire

1 Pryor, F. (2004). *Britain B.C.: life in Britain and Ireland before the Romans*. London: Harper Perennial, p.241.

Midmar Stone Circle, Aberdeenshire

1 Cope, J. (1998). *The Modern Antiquarian: a pre-millennial odyssey through megalithic Britain: including a gazetteer to over 300 prehistoric sites*. London: Thorsons, p.389.
2 Welfare, A. (2011). *Great Crowns of Stone: the recumbent stone circles of Scotland: gazetteer and appendices*. Edinburgh: RCAHMS, p.399. The full biblical quote is as follows: "That in the day that I shall visit the transgressions of Israel upon him I will also visit the altars of Bethel: and the horns of the altar shall be cut off, and fall to the ground." Amos 3:14.
3 See Hutton, R. (2014). *Pagan Britain*. New Haven; London: Yale University Press, pp.330–3.
4 Quoted in Burl, A. (2005). *A Guide to the Stone Circles of Britain, Ireland and Brittany*. New Haven; London: Yale University Press, p.104.
5 Stukeley, W. (1740). *Stonehenge: a temple restor'd to the British Druids*. London: W. Innys and R. Manby, p.2.
6 Lines, M. (2014). *The Traveller's Guide to Sacred Scotland*. Glastonbury: Gothic Image Publications, p.148.

The Hurlers, Cornwall

1 See Burnham, A. (ed.) (2018). *The Old Stones: a field guide to the megalithic sites of Britain and*

Ireland. London: Watkins.
2 See Thom, A. (1967). *Megalithic Sites in Britain*. Oxford: Clarendon Press.
3 Collins, W. (1861). *Rambles Beyond Railways*. London: Richard Bentley, p.43.
4 See Chorlton, A. (2019). *Cornish Folk Tales of Place*. Stroud: The History Press.

White Horse Hill, Oxfordshire
1 See Miles, D. (2019). *The Land of the White Horse: visions of England*. London: Thames & Hudson.
2 Ibid., p.106.

Coldrum Long Barrow, Kent
1 Cartwright, J. (1911). *The Pilgrims' Way from Winchester to Canterbury*. New York: E. P. Dutton and Company., p. 2
2 Bright, D. (2011). *The Pilgrims' Way: fact and fiction of an ancient trackway*. Stroud: The History Press.
3 Sullivan, D. (1999). *Ley Lines: a comprehensive guide to alignments*. London: Piatkus.
4 Heffernan, H. (2008). *Hop Pickers of Kent & Sussex*. Stroud: The History Press.
5 Simpson, J. and Roud, S. (2000). *A Dictionary of English Folklore*, p.186.

Abbots Bromley, Staffordshire
1 See Roud, S. (2008) in *The English Year: a month-by-month guide to the nation's customs and festivals, from May Day to Mischief Night*. London: Penguin Books, p.290.
2 Clark, C. (2014). "Playing the Stag in Medieval Middlesex? A perforated antler from South Mimms Castle – parallels and possibilities", in Baker, K., Carden, R. and Madgwick, R. (eds.) *Deer and People*. Oxford: Windgather Press, p.211.
3 Ibid.
4 Hutton, R. *The Stations of the Sun*, p.91.

The Rollright Stones, Oxfordshire
1 Larrington, C. (2019). *The Land of the Green Man: a journey through the supernatural landscapes of the British Isles*. London: Bloomsbury Academic, p.6.
2 Bloom, J. H. (1929). *Folk Lore, Old Customs and Superstitions in Shakespeare Land*. London: S.N., p.92.

3 Ibid., p.96.
4 See Waters, T. E. (2020). *Cursed Britain: a history of witchcraft and black magic in modern times*. New Haven: Yale University Press, p.197

Blakeney Point, Norfolk
1 See Bolt, R. (2012). *As Good as God, as Clever as the Devil: the impossible life of Mary Benson*. London: Atlantic.
2 *Ghost Stories* v08 n05 [1930-05]. (1930). [online] Internet Archive. Available at: https://archive.org/details/ghost-stories-v-08-n-05-1930-05/page/n1/mode/2up [Accessed 15 Aug. 2022].
3 Benson, E. F. (1928). *Spook Stories*. London: Hutchinson, p.121.
4 Ibid., p.111
5 See Lethbridge, T. C., and Wilson, W. (1985). *The Power of the Pendulum*. London: Arkana.
6 Benson, E. F. and Ashley, M. (2020). *The Outcast and Other Dark Tales* [Kindle version]. London: The British Library.

Ottery St Mary, Devon
1 See Groom, N. *The Seasons*, p.260.
2 Brand, J. (1849). *Observations on the Popular Antiquities of Great Britain: chiefly illustrating the origin of our vulgar and provincial customs, ceremonies, and superstitions*. London: Henry G. Bohn, p.389.
3 Hutton, R. *The Stations of the Sun*, p.364.
4 Foster, C. (2021). *Being a Human: adventures in 40,000 years of consciousness*. London: Profile Books, p.56.

The Devil's Quoits, Oxfordshire
1 Harte, J. (2009). "The Devil's Chapels: fiends, fear and folklore at prehistoric sites", in Parker, J. (ed.) *Written on Stone: the cultural history of British prehistoric monuments*. Newcastle: Cambridge Scholars.

Fernworthy Forest, Devon
1 Sandles, T. (2016). *Fernworthy Vengence Legendary Dartmoor*. [online] Available at: https://www.legendarydartmoor.co.uk/fern_venge.htm [Accessed 16 Oct. 2022].
2 Polwhele, R. (1793). *Historical Views of Devonshire in Five Volumes*. Vol. 1. Exeter: Cadell, Dilly & Murray, p.54.

3 See St. Leger-Gordon, R.E. (1973). *The Witchcraft and Folklore of Dartmoor*. Wakefield: EP Publishing, pp.30–1.

Dunwich, Suffolk
1 Fisher, M. (2016). *The Weird and the Eerie* [Kindle version]. London: Repeater Books.
2 Salusbury, M. (2021). *Matt Salusbury: Dunwich and climate change*. [online] Matt Salusbury. Available at: http://mattsalusbury.blogspot.com/2021/08/dunwich-and-climate-change.html [Accessed 14 Apr. 2022].
3 James, H. (1905). *English Hours*. Boston and New York: Houghton, Mifflin and Company, p.322.
4 Green, M. (2022). *Shadowlands: a journey through lost Britain*. London: Faber & Faber, p.166.

The Devil's Arrows, North Yorkshire
1 iniva. (2022). *News from the North by Emii Alrai*. [online] Available at: https://iniva.org/blog/2022/01/26/news-from-the-north-by-emii-alrai/ [Accessed 22 Aug. 2022].

Stonehenge, Wiltshire
1 See Geoffrey, Thompson, A. and Giles, J. A. (1842). *The British History of Geoffrey of Monmouth, in Twelve Books*. London: James Bohn.
2 Parker Pearson, M. (2021). "Archaeology and legend: investigating Stonehenge", *Archaeology International*, 24(1).
3 Parker Pearson, M., Pollard, J., Richards, C., Welham, K., Kinnaird, T., Shaw, D., Simmons, E., Stanford, A., Bevins, R., Ixer, R., Ruggles, C., Rylatt, J. and Edinborough, K. (2021). "The original Stonehenge? A dismantled stone circle in the Preseli Hills of west Wales", *Antiquity*, [online] 95(379), pp.85–103. [Accessed 16 Dec. 2022].
4 See Parker Pearson, M. (2014). *Stonehenge: a new understanding*. New York: The Experiment, pp.244–5.

Lud's Church, Staffordshire
1 Weston, J. L. and Crawford, M. M. (1904). *Sir Gawain and the Green Knight: a Middle-English Arthurian romance retold in modern prose: with introduction notes*. London: David Nutt, p.16.

2 Ibid., p. 17.
3 Armitage, S. (2007). *Sir Gawain and the Green Knight*. London: Faber & Faber, lines 2312–13.
4 Garner, A. and Elborough, T. (2006). *The Stone Book Quartet* [Kindle version]. London: Harper Perennial.

Burghead, Moray
1 See Noble, G. and Evans, N. (2019). *The King in the North: the Pictish realms of Fortriu and Ce*. Edinburgh: Birlinn.

Chepstow, Monmouthshire
1 See Hutton, R. *The Stations of the Sun*, p.46.
2 Owen, T. M. (2016). *The Customs and Traditions of Wales*. Cardiff: University of Wales Press, pp.56–7.

Silbury Hill, Wiltshire
1 Stukeley, W. (1743). *Abury, a Temple of the British Druids: with some others described . . . Volume the second*. London: W. Innys, R. Manby, B. Dod, J. Brindley, et al., p.101.
2 See Dames, M. (1977). *The Avebury Cycle*. London: Thames & Hudson.
3 Devereux, P. and Thomson, I. *The Ley Hunter's Companion*, pp.130–1.
4 Bayliss, A., McAvoy, F. and Whittle, A. (2007). "The World Recreated: redating Silbury Hill in its monumental landscape", *Antiquity*, 81(311), pp.26–53.
5 Whittle, A. (1997). *Sacred Mound, Holy Rings: Silbury Hill and the West Kennet palisade enclosures: a later Neolithic complex in north Wiltshire*. Oxford: Oxbow Books, p.166.
6 Michell, J. (1983). *The New View over Atlantis*. London: Thames and Hudson, p.213.

Trellech, Monmouthshire
1 See Main, L. (1995). *Walks in Mysterious Wales*. Wilmslow, Cheshire: Sigma Leisure, p. 128.

ADDITIONAL RESOURCES

calendarcustoms.com
This site provides an overview of traditional events across the UK. It's especially useful for checking what's on and when.

efdss.org
The English Folk Dance and Song Society promotes the folk arts across England. The Society's London home, Cecil Sharp House, hosts regular gigs, dances and classes.

folkloremythmagic.com
The Centre for Folklore, Myth and Magic in Todmorden, West Yorkshire hosts exhibitions and events on a range of topics of interest to the weird walker. The venue also has its own tea room, library and folklore shop.

megalithic.co.uk
The Megalithic Portal is a goldmine of information about ancient sites. The accompanying app allows you to discover all kinds of interesting spots you never knew existed.

museumofwitchcraftandmagic.co.uk
Boscastle's Museum of Witchcraft and Magic houses a unique collection of artefacts related to British magical practice. Situated in a beautiful Cornish fishing port, it's a must-visit for weird walkers.

ordnancesurvey.co.uk
The Ordnance Survey app (OS Maps Premium) is a great way to plan routes inspired by the walking notes in this book.

righttoroam.org.uk
Right to Roam is campaigning to extend the Countryside and Rights of Way Act in England so that millions more people can have easy access to open space and the physical, mental and spiritual health benefits that it brings.

themodernantiquarian.com
Based on Julian Cope's classic megalithic guidebook, this site is a wonderful and ever-expanding resource.

wegooutsidetoo.com
We Go Outside Too aims to make the British countryside more accessible to the Black community and promote the many benefits associated with exploring the natural world.

woodlandtrust.org.uk
The Woodland Trust website features a useful month-by-month guide to sustainable foraging. The site also includes some good recipes to try out with your foraged harvest.

INDEX